THE
LOVE DIARY
of
A

ZULU
Boy

A MEMOIR

Bhekisisa Mncube

PENGUIN BOOKS

Published by Penguin Books
an imprint of Penguin Random House South Africa (Pty) Ltd
Reg. No. 1953/000441/07
The Estuaries No. 4, Oxbow Crescent, Century Avenue, Century City, 7441
PO Box 1144, Cape Town, 8000, South Africa
www.penguinrandomhouse.co.za

Penguin
Random House
South Africa

First published 2018

1 3 5 7 9 10 8 6 4 2

Publication © Penguin Books 2018
Text © Bhekisisa Mncube 2018

Cover image: floral illustrations © shutterstock/Nebula Cordata

PUBLISHER: Marlene Fryer
MANAGING EDITOR: Ronel Richter-Herbert
EDITOR: Angela Voges
PROOFREADER: Ronel Richter-Herbert
COVER DESIGNER: Monique Cleghorn
TEXT DESIGNER: Ryan Africa
TYPESETTER: Monique Cleghorn

Set in 11 pt on 16 pt Minion

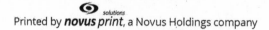

Printed by **novus print**, a Novus Holdings company

MIX
Paper from
responsible sources
FSC® C022948

Penguin Random House is committed to a sustainable
future for our business, our readers and our planet.
This book is made from Forest Stewardship Council ® certified paper.

Disclaimer
Some names and identifying details have been changed to protect the privacy of individuals.

ISBN 978 1 77609 280 2 (print)
ISBN 978 1 77609 281 9 (ePub)

Contents

Author's note

Dear reader, thank you very much for buying and reading this book. My name is Bhekisisa Mncube. The shortened version of my name is Bheki. In political circles, I was nicknamed Stalin. In English, the name Bhekisisa literally translated means 'you must be vigilant'. However, this name does not appear in any of my official records – not even my birth and baptismal certificates. In official records, I am simply recorded as Walter Mncube. Although she is illiterate, my mother admitted in 2015 that she had given me the English name Walter. (I learnt later in life that Walter is, in fact, a German name.) All my siblings were given English or European names accordingly, in keeping with my mother's wishes. However, my mother's child-naming regime must be understood within the overall context of the time. Blacks were routinely given English or European names by priests, teachers and white employers; the late revered statesman President Nelson Rolihlahla Mandela was given his English name on his first day of school – by a teacher.

This book is a romance memoir. It is a fable of lust, love, sex, obsession, loss, friendship, betrayal and fantasy. At times, it's erotic, romantic and tragic. At others, it's comical. It is inspired by the real-life drama of a deepening romantic relationship between a Zulu boy and an Englishwoman. Thus, its main theme is a compelling look at intimate interracial relationships in modern-day South Africa.

The relationship under the microscope has stood the test of time. Its seed was planted in the trenches of the African National Congress (ANC) underground in the early 1990s, and it found its feet in the new South Africa. In a series of diary entries, the book takes us on a whirlwind tour of this seventeen-year-old relationship, which has survived the Zulu cultural demands for the slaughter of a cow to introduce an Englishwoman to the Zulu ancestors; four weddings; and an imagined yet troublesome foursome involving a proverbial gardener, Thabo, and the Pool and Bean Boys.

The Love Diary of a Zulu Boy is a lurch across the racial divide that triggers memories of a plethora of failed romantic affairs, including bizarre details about love spells, wet dreams, infidelity, sexually transmitted diseases, phantom pregnancies, sexless relationships, threesomes, prostitution and a polyandrous love affair that went south. Interwoven in the stories is the transformation of intimacy in post-apartheid South Africa. Seasoned journalist and author of six books, including *Dancing the Death Drill*, Fred Khumalo, describes this book thus: 'The book goes beyond being a narrative of forbidden love. It's a potent alchemy, a swirling together of matters that are the hallmark of serious literature: good and evil, sex, love, friendship, morality, happiness and suffering, heroes and villains, betrayal, and, of course, the old South African chestnuts – race and identity.'

I hope you will enjoy reading it as much as I did writing it.

Foreword

STEPHANIE SAVILLE, DEPUTY EDITOR AT
THE WITNESS NEWSPAPER

For me, a good piece of writing often delivers a gasp factor. It's that moment when the reader hits the golden nugget of the story, which elicits either an audible or cerebral gasp. It's when something inside you inhales quickly because of extreme emotion – joy, horror, fascination or any myriad of others. Prepare to gasp as you turn the pages of this collection of short stories. If you are anything like me, you'll love every minute of looking inside at some of what makes this extraordinary writer tick.

Bheki Mncube and I had a lot of fun recently as we embarked on the exciting task of disseminating some of his very personal memoir-type writing to readers of *The Witness* newspaper.

Writing this, it occurred to me that Bheki and I have actually met face to face only a few times. Although he had been at *The Witness* in various guises over some years, this was before I had arrived at the newspaper. But while I was working as a journalist in Pietermaritzburg, I would come across him in his capacity as a spin doctor and chat to him at various jobs. I admit to having, at times, been a bit in awe of him. He always really seemed to know his stuff and was confident to the point of giving off a slightly cocky air. Although I never really knew him that well, I have realised, through exposure to some of his innermost thoughts in the form of these stories, that these were probably rather astute observations.

I forget exactly how this project started, but it involved liaising with our features editor, Linda Longhurst, to get Bheki's byline back into *The Witness*, and I think Facebook was the proper genesis. If my memory serves me correctly, it was a tongue-in-cheek post by Stalin – for that was how I first knew Bheki – which dealt with the antics of Thabo, his gardener.

Thabo seemed to constantly irk Bheki, and it seemed the more irritated he got with Thabo, the more his wife, the lovely Professor D., came to Thabo's rescue. Bheki wrote about this in a wonderfully facetious style, feigning great jealousy for the hapless gardener who seemed to have usurped his wife's affections. It made me giggle, because I could relate so well. At home, I defend our gardener all the time. I, like the adored wife of Stalin, am the one who speaks up for him and makes light of his foibles. Who cannot but be extremely fond of the man who keeps one's external – and in our case, often internal – home environment in check?

As Stalin's posts about Thabo hit Facebook, many of his Facebook followers picked sides, mostly giving Thabo their full empathy. The more we defended Thabo, the more Bheki feigned venom towards him and the more humorous his posts became. I, like many others I'm sure, began to look forward to seeing the next instalment; commenting often on them, I saw how many others loved hearing about Thabo's antics. Often, Bheki would post something disparaging about Thabo and there would be a clamour of comments leaping to the gardener's defence. At some point, I commented that he should write a column about Thabo for *The Witness* and, happily, Bheki obliged. But he did not stop there: more columns, to our great delight, followed.

I was pleased because Bheki is well known to most of our long-time readers, having worked as a reporter and columnist at *The Witness* in the early 2000s. It was wonderful to be offering our readers some light relief that was also often thought-provoking and, at times, pleasingly off-beat. I became slightly fascinated by the style of Bheki's writing. It is open, honest, gritty and, on occasion, pretty sensual. In fact, some of it was too hot for our readers and, after one particular piece which Linda and I felt was fine, we realised we had to decline some of the more steamy pieces, as a couple of older readers complained.

Bheki's writing is a glimpse into or a snapshot of life from the vantage point of one who has had many varied, rich experiences, keenly felt (or not), which many would know nothing about. And some of those snapshots were so far removed from the experience of many of our readers that I felt they provided a window to another world, one which would enrich our lives if we took the time to read about it.

With Bheki's writing, there is no sanitising of emotions or any hiding from the darker aspects of experience. In these stories, the reader will find he tells it like it is. What makes this appealing is that we can often relate on a more personal, often more visceral, level if the writer is honest. And honest he seems to be.

While he can be nonchalant and almost swaggers through the pages at times, Bheki also readily admits his inner conflict, guilt and regret – for example, for the way he has used women in the past. He tells his story, lays it bare, and then, just as you're seething on behalf of the poor woman he has used so wrongly, he admits his guilt. The schoolgirl he hit, the prostitute, the young woman he nonchalantly deflowered. His regret is important, because it elicits sympathy both for the wronged and the now-ashamed wrongdoer.

I believe that his experience as a journalist is important in his writing, because he gets to the point of his stories pretty fast, which is important for a short-story writer, offering a tale in rich colour, in a limited space.

For me, his wife, Professor D., attains a near-holy status. She is clearly so adored by this man. And, in this relationship, we see the incurable romantic that Bheki is. He allows this white woman – for, while she is said to have no time for her race label, he mentions it rather often – to run circles around him. I have yet to meet her. What does she think? Who taught her to handle men so marvellously? And can she teach us?

There is, at times, a rather thrilling experience to be had from the stories. And this is not meant in a voyeuristic sense. His encounter with a prostitute – 'an absolutely horror-filled experience' – is so brutally honest that it arouses respect for the telling of it. Here, again, his admission of guilt and shame about paying for sex suffuses the pages.

What is intriguing for the female reader is that there is often a strange curiosity about the way male sexuality works. How do men experience the interplay of the sexes, and what does it all mean to them? There is an underlying fascination with male sexuality. Where women will often agonise over a sexual encounter, men's perceived bravado about it all is somewhat fascinating.

These stories have clearly been important for Bheki to tell. Some are set far in the past. Is there something cathartic about writing about them now? Will it help him that others will now know about them? What is clear is that these experiences have changed Bheki.

He is not the Bheki of high school, or the hopeless down-and-out, or the Bheki at tertiary education.

I find his quiet sagacity inspiring, like his quote: 'It is therefore my contention that we need to re-imagine the tired concepts of apartheid-fuelled race identity and racial profiling. We are human beings before the socially constructed notion of race. Let us love and let us live.'

And, I would add, let us gasp, for whatever reason, so we can know that we live.

AUTHOR Q&A WITH STEPHANIE SAVILLE

Why do you write?

I write to unburden myself. The genesis of my writing journey was 1993, after the brutal killing of South African Communist Party (SACP) general secretary and struggle stalwart Chris Hani. At the time, I was registered for Communication in English A. The lecturer had volunteered her time for all those who wanted to improve their writing in English. I grasped that opportunity with both hands, and then boom! Comrade Hani was killed. I wrote ten pages filled with vitriol on the effects of Hani's death. Despite the general doom and gloom that pervaded the nation, after writing my thoughts down I felt I could handle the untimely demise of my hero.

The second time writing saved me was when I underwent trauma counselling in 2006 to deal with the negative effects my father had had on my upbringing. The psychologist asked me to write a letter to my father and tell him how I felt about him. I wrote over ten pages – unburdening my emotions, as it were. She read my letter and used it as a basis for further therapeutic work. As a result of that therapeutic work, I accepted my family name, Bhekisisa, which I hated because it reminded me of my father. If you check *The Witness* newspaper archives, I wrote under the byline Bheki Ka Mncube. So, writing for me is part of my own therapy to heal from the wounds of the past. Since 2006, I have written under the byline Bhekisisa Mncube.

But, why write a romance memoir? Is it an act of bravado?
Certainly, it is not an act of bravado. These memoirs are actually an apology to women I have wronged. It is an apology for the half a man that I was. I am no longer the man I grew up as. This romance memoir is to say that I am not my father. My father treated women badly. He managed to father twenty-one known children with a variety of women, although he remained married only to my mother. My mother only gave birth to seven of the twenty-one children. For the longest time, my love life mimicked that of my father, except that I was lucky I didn't father numerous children. In this collection, my father's misogynistic and patriarchal tendencies are laid bare. I am doing it to let go of the past. I am writing to free myself from the man I was. It is a statement of intent to say, since I have found true love and learnt to be a real man, this is how I deal with my not-so-cosy past.

I then decided to document my experiences. None of it is flattering. I am opening myself into the world to be judged and mocked. I am ready for this. But, deep down in my heart, I know I owe these women an apology. The best I can do is to admit to having been a Casanova. My inspiration is drawn from André Brink's book, *Before I Forget*. He wrote beautifully about all the women he ever loved. The point, really, is to humanise the ones who fell prey to the sexual predator. The grand idea is to give these women recognition – to name them, so that they can assume their rightful place in history – not as statistics, but as real people.

How have you managed to stay the course in writing this memoir?
The reason I have stayed the course is, of course, my wife and daughter. Neither of them know who I was before I received therapy and got the monkey off my back, as it were. I am a new man. I am a man of rational thoughts and rational actions, but it was not always like this. I want my son to know how not to treat women – learning from my past experiences and anecdotal evidence about his grandfather. The chapter called 'True love: True betrayal and a baby boy' is about my relationship with my son's mother.

What effect has recording these memories in writing had on you, as you wrote them and as people read them?
I feel a great sense of freedom. I write things that people would never put in print. It is a process of renewal so that I can look back and say, Yes, I have wronged women, but here I am, fighting to remain a new man. Since this process began three years ago, I have become acutely aware of my own human frailty. I somehow feel that I survived so that I can tell the tale. Explain to me how come I never got the dreaded HIV/AIDS virus, with so many girlfriends parked in the same lane? There must have been a greater purpose. I want to look at myself in the mirror and say, I like what I have become. I am not a prisoner of my past. My past cannot determine my future. Basically, the message is that, despite growing up in an environment that perpetuated patriarchy, one's own agency can be deployed to change the course of one's life.

And is there any feeling of vulnerability in writing about your conquests, or is it all male bravado?
I feel completely naked. I feel judged already. Yet, I feel that I can finally live with myself. I sleep better at night.

Prologue

I was born an ugly embryo, my face covered in a white veil, caul or hood. The *Caput galeatum*, a membrane covering the newborn, is called *ukuzalwa wembethe* in isiZulu. According to isiZulu lore, being born with a veil is a sign of special destiny and psychic abilities, or good luck. I am yet to reap the benefits of *ukuzalwa ngembethe*. Just kidding: I am, indeed, a special kid. I possess psychic powers that work mainly through dreams. (There is a chapter that explores this in the book.)

I was born in apartheid South Africa, black and poor. My future was blighted from the start. My parents were poverty-stricken and disfranchised. I inherited, through the accident of my birth, the intergenerational chains of poverty.

My family was so poor that *sasidla imbuya ngothi*: literally translated, we were eating grass with a stick, living in abject poverty. Going hungry was routine. My father did odd jobs in the local white towns of Eshowe and Empangeni. When I was much younger, I am told – in 1979 or thereabouts – he worked as general labourer when the University of Zululand was extended. He would ride 68.5 kilometres on a bicycle to and from work. At one stage, he earned R9.99 per month as a night-time security guard working for a hardware store.

Later, he found a job at a local farm, then worked as a security guard again. In these trying circumstances, my mother had to chip in and do some handiwork, such as making Zulu mats (*amacansi*).

My early memories of our eating habits – when we had any food at all – go as follows. We would eat porridge with salt instead of sugar for breakfast. For lunch, we would always have dried beans and *uphuthu*, a form of starch made from maize meal. *Uphuthu* is often eaten with meat, beans, gravy and/or sour milk. Sometimes, we would have sour milk for lunch, if there were cows to be milked. For dinner, we would have *imifino* (the edible part of a wild, leafy plant). We loved one particular type, known as *imbuya*.

The problem was that all this was seasonal. Sour milk depended on cow's milk, while *imifino* could only be harvested in summer after good rains. Compounding the problem was, of course, lack of money, so most of the time we would run out of sugar, salt, cooking oil and maize meal, even if we had *imifino* and sour milk. It is here where the Zulu tradition of *ukwenana* came through for us. *Ukwenana* is a cultural form of exchange in which the recipient accepts, intending to reciprocate in kind, but the giver engages in the action knowing that there may not, in fact, be reciprocation. In simple language, we were traditional food beggars. We suffered from chronic hunger.

In my household, there was no time to rest; we always had tasks to perform. In winter, my mother kept a small garden that boasted vegetables and greens such as cabbage, spinach, onions, tomatoes, beans and beetroot. We had to help her with this garden by fetching water for irrigation three kilometres away from the homestead. We used wheelbarrows to transport each twenty-five-litre container of water, and had to repeat this at least four times daily. My father later procured fifty-litre containers; while they were heavier, they made our job easier, as they halved the number of times we had to go to the dam to fetch water. In summer, we farmed maize and pumpkins. Luckily, these never needed irrigation, as they depended on good rains. However, before dawn during the weed season, we would be out in the fields – mainly the maize fields – weeding; after sunrise, we would take the extended family's herd of cattle for grazing. The irony, of course, is that my father didn't own any livestock.

Seasonally speaking, summer was good for us – special, even, as we fed on *amakhowe*. *Amakhowe* is the isiZulu word for a species of indigenous edible mushroom that grows wild in subtropical habitats in southern Africa. Unfortunately, even then, the weather had to play a special part – we needed a bit of thunder and rain. Within hours of a soaking shower and thunderstorm, the *amakhowe* started to germinate, and the hunt would begin immediately. For some strange reason, if not harvested immediately, this delicacy would disappear.

My umbilical cord lies buried deep in the bowels of the earth in the small town of Eshowe in the province of KwaZulu-Natal, South Africa. I hail from the rural hinterland of the northern part of the KwaZulu-Natal province, near the town of Eshowe, in the village called eHabeni (a place of hyperbole). The village is settled in the rugged, poverty-stricken area bordering the formerly white towns of Eshowe and Empangeni. My humble home, built of stones and sand, fell under the traditional leadership authority of Inkosi Sam Mhlaba, a Zulu prince from the same royal house as the reigning king of the Zulu nation, His Majesty King Goodwill Zwelithini KaBhekuzulu. The village took its name from the name of the *isigodlo* (palace) of the Zulu royal Inkosi Bhekeshowe, father of Inkosi Mhlaba. It was officially known as Mbangathubane, overlook-

ing the majestic mountains of Mpehlela near another village called
uMhlathuzane. We would bathe in the local river, the Amatheku,
which runs through the village. I started and completed my primary-
school education at Habeni Primary School. Subsequently, I completed my high-school education at the Bhekeshowe High School,
named after Inkosi Mhlaba's father Inkosi Bhekeshowe.

Both my village of eHabeni and my town of Eshowe feature
prominently in the epic events of Zulu history. This is where the
founder of the Zulu nation, the legendary King Shaka Zulu, had his
slaughterhouse for delinquents, known as KwaBulawayo. Eshowe also
features prominently in the praises of King Cetshwayo kaMpande
(the last king of the independent Zulu nation, from 1872 to 1879),
which relay that he travelled from KwaMaqwakazi (a village near
eHabeni) via the grand Mpehlela mountains to Ulundi (the capital of the erstwhile Zulu Kingdom). History records that King
Cetshwayo kaMpande was born at Mlambongwenya, near Eshowe.
Coincidentally, in 1981, my father was asked by the KwaZulu Legislative Assembly (the homeland or Bantustan government of the
time) and the Zulu royal family to rebuild King Cetshwayo's *isigodlo*,
which was destroyed by the British army in the Battle of Ulundi
on 4 July 1879.

Today, the KwaZulu Cultural Museum at Ondini, and the site of
King Cetshwayo's royal palace, stand tall on the same ground upon
which the murderous British army had walked silently in the dead
of night to burn the palace down after their historic defeat by the
mighty Zulu army at the Battle of Isandlwana on 22 January 1879.

Eshowe's elevated position on a hilltop overlooking the hot and
humid Zululand coastal plain gives the town its cool serenity, but the
Dlinza Forest, around which the town wraps itself, gives Eshowe its

soul, or so say the post-apartheid tourism brochures about my town. Tourism authorities contend that no other town in South Africa has blended so organically into its environment. Blessed with the abundant natural diversity around them, Eshowe residents boast that there is a flower in a tree every day of the year in their town. This lush environment and refreshing climate has always attracted human habitation, and no fewer than four Zulu kings have, at some point, called Eshowe their home.

Unfortunately, the Mncubes inhabited a part of Eshowe that was reserved for 'surplus people' after the apartheid government passed the Group Areas Act on 27 April 1950. For political novices, this means barren rural land was meant for black people only, as the Group Areas Act determined land settlement by the colour of one's skin. The fertile and beautiful parts of South Africa were snatched from black people and reserved for white people only. There was absolutely nothing lush about my village. We fetched water from streams, rivers and dams, competing with livestock. There were no tarred roads and no electricity. The land was desolate. To illustrate the extent of the desolation, let me turn to Alan Paton, writing in his vintage book, *Cry, the Beloved Country:*

> The great red hills stand desolate, and the earth has torn away like flesh. The lightning flashes over them, the clouds pour down upon them, the dead streams come to life, full of the red blood of the earth. Down in the valleys women scratch the soil that is left, and the maize hardly reaches the height of a man. They are valleys of old men and old women, of mothers and children. The men are away, the young men and girls are away. The soil cannot keep them any more.

My village couldn't retain young men; most headed for Johannesburg or Durban as soon as they passed puberty, to look for jobs without having completed either primary or secondary education.

Of the Mncube clan in eHabeni village, consisting of some nine households with over fifty young men and women, only my mother's children broke two records – first household to have a matriculant, and the first one to boast a university graduate. Today, the children of MaMlambo (my mother's maiden name) boast no fewer than six degrees and three national diplomas.

I am a true farm boy. I grew up tilling the land that was meant to sustain my family – three brothers and four sisters, and my mother and father. But it never did. I spent my formative years as a cattle herder, despite the fact that my father had no cattle.

In the year I was born, South Africa held another whites-only general election. The 1974 election was called a year earlier than required by law. The National Party (NP) swept to victory again, which meant that Prime Minister John Vorster, fervent supporter of apartheid South Africa, was returned to power. In that year, the NP regime declared Afrikaans a medium of instruction alongside English in all schools. Black students began to mobilise themselves; the regime would come to regret this decision barely two years later.

Interestingly, I was born a year after the ground-breaking event commonly referred to as the Durban Strikes, in which thousands of workers downed tools. When black workers in Durban embarked on a wave of strikes in January 1973, the government and employers were shocked, and they responded mainly by giving in to the workers' demands. Thus began a resurgence of union activity that would culminate in the formation of the massive trade union federations that helped in the arduous process of dismantling apartheid by the late 1980s.

Hardly two years after my birth, the historic 1976 Soweto Uprising happened. According to South African History Online, the uprising,

> which began in the Gauteng township famously known as Soweto and spread countrywide, profoundly changed the socio-political landscape in South Africa. Events that triggered the uprising can be traced back to policies of the apartheid regime that resulted in the introduction of the Bantu Education Act in 1953. The rise of the Black Consciousness Movement (BCM) and the formation of South African Students Organisation (SASO) raised the political consciousness of many students while others joined the wave of anti-apartheid sentiment within the student community. [...] On 16 June 1976, between 3 000 and 10 000 students mobilised by the Soweto Students Representative Council's Action Committee supported by the BCM marched peacefully to demonstrate and protest against the government's directive. The march was meant to culminate at a rally in Orlando Stadium.
>
> On their pathway they were met by heavily armed police who fired teargas and later live ammunition on demonstrating students. This resulted in a widespread revolt that turned into an uprising against the regime. While the uprising began in Soweto, it spread across the country and carried on until the following year.

My birth during this tumultuous political climate prepared me for a life of political struggle. At the tender age of twelve, I joined the anti-apartheid forces led by the African National Congress Mission in Exile.

———

The year 1981, when I turned seven, was an eventful one. In January, according to historical records, the guerrillas from the ANC's military wing, Umkhonto we Sizwe (MK), attacked the Koeberg nuclear power plant in Cape Town. In the same month, the United Nations Special Committee against Apartheid launched the International Year of Mobilisation for Sanctions against South Africa. These events may have had no bearing on the mundane life of eHabeni, but something epic was about to happen in the Mncube family, which would define my relationship with my father for the rest of my life.

Here is how the story unfolded. My peers routinely started school when they turned seven. Somehow, I realised that I had been left behind. I raised the matter with my mother. She said, '*Ey Mntanami uyihlo akafuni* (Ey, my son, your father says no schooling for you as you're still very young).' I protested that all my peers were at school and that my right arm could already touch my left ear without me bending my neck. You see, that was an important test to establish whether you were ready to start school – while standing straight, your right arm had to touch your left ear, no neck-bending. My mother suggested that I raise the matter directly with my father. She could no longer play intermediary, as all her previous attempts had been rebuffed.

I immediately seized upon the challenge. At the time, my father was working night shift at some hardware store in Eshowe. My plan was simple – as soon as he arrived home the next morning, I would confront him. The stage was set. I was angry. Scratch that: I was seething with rage. I was ready for my first epic battle to escape the meaninglessness of life in eHabeni village. My father arrived the next day, as usual, at about 8 a.m. Usually, he would arrive home and my mother would brew some hot tea for him. He would have the tea, then sleep for a few hours. While he was drinking his tea, I pounced. No pleasantries! No warning!

'Father, I am going to start school tomorrow, like all my peers. And Father, don't worry about the uniform, you can organise that later. Mom said she has twenty cents from the saucer for school fees.'

You see, my mother had a saucer for donations, as she was a faith healer. Consultations were free, but one had to bring a white candle – or pay twenty cents in lieu of one if you couldn't bring a candle. As part of *Ubuntu*, most patients donated some money after their sickness riddle had been solved. My mom's main job as a faith healer was to intercede with the ancestors so that they could explain the reason for the sickness in the family, or any other conundrum confronting the family.

After I had surprised my father with my announcement, I was in a hurry to disappear, as I feared his fury. He stood there, frozen in the moment. He looked like he had seen a ghost. As I prepared to leave, he said, '*Ayi kuyezwakala* (I hear you).' He never uttered the words, 'It's okay, you can go to school.' Nonetheless, I left in a jiffy to report to my mom that he had agreed. I was not about to bore her with the finer details of our conversation, if you could call it that.

By the time he came home the next morning, I was already at school.

For me, school was a sort of escape. I wasn't sure if schooling had the potential to transform the substance of my life, or just the contours. But one thing was for sure: I wanted to be at school and as far away from cattle-herding as I could get. By the time I turned five, it had occurred to me that the art of cattle-herding was, in fact, a study in patience, solitude and nothingness – none of the skills I had mastered or had any desire to excel at. I wanted to learn. I wanted to read and write like my big brother.

9

Interviewed for this book, my mother remembers the incident as if it had occurred just yesterday.

'Your father came back from work in the morning as usual. He asked about your whereabouts. I said you had gone to school,' she recalls.

What happened next would shock the entire extended Mncube clan. My father flew into a fit of rage. In a one-man shouting match, he accused my mother of disrespect and gross misconduct, and said a whole lot of other, unprintable, stuff. In the aftermath of his rage, he refused to eat the food that she had prepared for him. This act alone is severe censure for a misbehaving wife. Then, he went on to report my mother's alleged gross misconduct to his elder brother – uMahlaleshushu. In the Zulu traditional family set-up, reporting your wife to the elders is the ultimate form of showing that you're pissed off and that you expect the elders to mete out appropriate punishment upon your misbehaving wife. It calls for the whole clan to intervene to break the impasse. In some cases, it may lead to the wife being suspended from her wifely duties – meaning, sent back to her maiden home. She would only be allowed to return with an appropriate apology, accompanied by her elders. In these situations, it is compulsory to slaughter a goat to apprise the ancestors of the *ukukhumelana umlotha* (peace-making) ritual.

My mother escaped this severe censure but, within days of my father reporting her, she appeared before a hastily convened disciplinary committee headed by Mahlaleshushu and consisting of other senior members of the Mncube clan. My mother faced a charge of conduct unbecoming a good Zulu wife. In her plea, she protested her innocence, apparently reminding my father that he had told her years earlier to decide the appropriate age for their children to start school.

To cut a long story short, my mother was reprimanded for her actions and told never to repeat her despicable behaviour. Apparently, Mahlaleshushu later confided to my mother that he had seen nothing wrong with her actions. As the storm raged about me starting school, I was oblivious to the full magnitude of my actions and the trouble I had got my mother into. As they say, the rest is history. I was not recalled from school. Later, a semblance of normality returned to our household. But my relationship with my father had entered the first phase of its slippery slope.

My mother says the ancestors communicated with her and were angered by my father's actions. He apparently owes me an apology. At the time of writing, she had still not told my father about the ancestors' demand. The reason? She still fears my father's fury.

My second confrontation with my father was more dramatic. According to my diary entry, it occurred on 1 January 1993: 'My father refuse [*sic*] to give me money to further my studies.'

Dear reader, let me take you back to that fateful day on Friday 1 January 1993. The Matric results for 1992 had been published a few days earlier. I had seen my name in the *Ilanga* newspaper and knew I had passed. Since the announcement, I had been in a state of ecstasy. I knew that – at last – I was about to leave the village of eHabeni for good. I was armed with a bursary, awarded by the Ecumenical Bursary Fund, that would enable me to study further. I was almost certain of my future, until I broached the subject with my father:

Me: Father, as you know, I have passed Matric. I will further my studies, possibly in law. I have really been lucky to have been awarded a bursary. I request that you give me some money for travelling and food.

Father: Are you mad? I have made a plan for you to join the KwaZulu Police and start working to earn a living. I have already spoken to Mr Dladla. Do you think I have a bottomless pit of money just for you? You're old enough now to have to chip in and help educate your sisters. Mina, I have a new wife to take. I have put my plans on hold all these years. There will be no money from my pocket for any further studies. Do you understand?

Me: But Father, I can't be a KwaZulu Police officer. These people are killers. I want to be a lawyer and I will be – with or without your permission.

Father: You do as you please, son. I gave you an opportunity and you threw it back in my face. Let's see if your Mandela will educate you. Now, if you'll excuse me?'

Me: But Father …

He did not wait for me to finish, and walked out of his own house.

On Sunday 3 January 1993, my father left for Ulundi, where he worked. He had not spoken to me since our ugly spat. According to my diary, I left eHabeni for Durban on 12 January and neither saw nor spoke to my father for the rest of the year. Needless to say, something in me died that day. I could not believe that my own father did not share in my ambition to be the first in the whole Mncube clan to acquire a higher-education qualification. What irked me the most is that he wanted to take a second wife, despite the fact that we were struggling financially at home.

———

In the annals of South African history, 1986 was an epic year. The apartheid government declared its second state of emergency and thousands of activists were either arrested or killed in running battles with apartheid forces. The first state of emergency had been declared on 21 July 1985; it clearly did not have the desired effect, as townships continued to erupt in sporadic riots and marches. The United Democratic Front (UDF) asserted itself through a series of low-key acts of defiance, such as rent boycotts, labour strikes and school stayaways.

Only my late brother (Bhekuyise, 'Big Bheki') and my father ever bothered about politics. Bhekuyise had an ambivalent relationship with the ANC and believed strongly in self-help and African pride. He used to collect banned materials for his reading pleasure, which he later passed on to me. So, my political education started at home. He also fiddled with the radio a lot in the 1980s. I later learnt that he was picking up Radio Freedom, the propaganda arm of the ANC during the anti-apartheid struggle from the 1970s to the 1990s. It was the oldest liberation radio station in Africa. Listening to Radio Freedom was a revolutionary act in South Africa: the apartheid government viewed it as an act of treason and it was punishable by imprisonment.

It came as no surprise to me, then, that in 1986 I performed my first political act by snubbing Inkatha Yenkululeko Yesizwe (today's Inkatha Freedom Party) and withholding the fifty cents meant for its membership. For the most part of its existence as a political party, Inkatha Yenkululeko Yesizwe was the sole leader of the Kwa-Zulu Legislative Assembly, created by the Self-governing Territories Constitution Act, 1971, during the apartheid years. A year earlier, the apartheid regime had passed the Black Homelands Citizenship Act, 1970, which formally designated all black South Africans as citizens of the homelands (even if they lived in 'white South Africa') and cancelled their South African citizenship.

For some odd reason, Inkatha leader Mangosuthu Gatsha Buth-elezi had decreed that all people living under the patronage of the

KwaZulu homeland had to be members of Inkatha. On top of that, all learners throughout the self-governing territory had to study a subject known as *Ubuntu Botho* – essentially political education, heavily tinged with the alleged heroics of Buthelezi and his illegitimate government, but largely considered Inkatha propaganda lessons. These were held once a week on Thursdays.

Dear reader, let me now take you back to that specific mundane Thursday at Habeni Primary School in 1986. In *Ubuntu Botho* class, the teacher distributed Inkatha membership forms. We were all asked to write our names on them and sign them. When you returned the form, you had to pay fifty cents. Although my mother gave me seventy cents to join Inkatha and buy some sweets with the change, I had decided against such a move, having my misgivings about this yearly donation.

I decided to inquire more about the nature and form of this beast called Inkatha. My inquiries revealed what I had suspected since 1983: that Inkatha was not a liberation movement, but part of the oppressor. You may recall that 20 August 1983 marked the birth of the UDF, an anti-apartheid body that incorporated many anti-apartheid organisations but excluded Inkatha. I had gleaned from Bhekuyise's newspaper clippings that the UDF represented over 600 civic groups, churches, and student and youth organisations, which made it a real people's movement. I pestered many a family member to explain to me why Inkatha was not part of the UDF, but to no avail. So, 1986 was a coming of age for me – my first political initiation. I had reached political consciousness and picked a corner – that of the anti-apartheid forces led by the ANC Mission in Exile. I decided right there and then to defy Inkatha, my school and my mother.

On that specific Thursday, dear reader, I returned the Inkatha membership form half-filled out, with no money. The teacher, a

Mr Cebekhulu, inquired as to the dues. I said, in perfect Zulu: '*Ngiyaxolisa thisha ayikho imali ekhaya, njalonje silala singadlile. Ngakhoke angeke ngikwazi ukusebenzisa imali yesinkwa ukujoyina iqembu lezombusazwe.* (I am sorry, Sir, we don't have money at home; mostly we sleep on an empty stomach, so I can't use bread money to join a political party).'

The teacher was stunned, but let it slide. I won the day. Later in my life, this decision would further strain my relationship with my father.

In 2004, I wrote about this incident in my *Witness/Echo* column: 'My 50 cents' worth of advice is that the IFP must close shop to save itself political embarrassment.'

———

I was not sad when my father died. I did not mourn his death. In fact, I had a sense of ecstasy once the funeral ceremony had concluded. I know it sounds absurd and frankly callous for a boy child not to feel pain when his father dies, but I did not and still wouldn't, even if given a second chance. In fact, I will not feel any pain anytime soon, if I can help it.

Truth is, I killed my father. Yes, I had to kill my father to survive the Mncubes' malady: mental illness. My psychologist helped me commit the ultimate crime. My father was murdered in what my psychologist and I described as a mercy killing. The idea emerged while I was sitting comfortably on the Freudian couch with my psychologist. She was talking non-stop, trying to console me; I was weeping uncontrollably.

This is how the story goes. I suffered a nervous or mental breakdown in 2006. Instead of being sent to a traditional hospital ward, my physician, a Dr Parag, had me committed to the loony bin at the Entabeni Hospital in Durban. A psychologist came to see me in my ward – not really a ward, but a facility where people of my kind had to spend time with themselves, 'to unwind'. It was full of nerds, elites, educationists, alcoholics, druggies, chartered accountants and former business executives – all suffering from a malady of life. In medical terms, it's called depression. I was diagnosed with clinical depression. This, for me, was not a new diagnosis. I had first encountered the words 'clinical depression' in 1996, when I was a student leader at what was then Technikon Natal (now the Durban University of Technology). Clearly, the condition had worsened over the years because it had not been treated.

As part of my psychotherapy, the psychologist suggested that I write a letter to my father to express my dismay at the manner in which he had treated me, my mom and my siblings over the years. I wrote over ten pages. I submitted it the next day. After reading my vitriol, she asked whether I could go home and read it to my father. I said no. As far as I was concerned, my father was beyond redemption. This is how the idea of killing my father was born. She advised me to cut all ties with him immediately. In dramatic fashion, she said: 'You must just kill your father and move on with your life.' She explained to me that, because I was not prepared to forgive my father, I had to kill him before he died a natural death. She explained the process thus: 'Take this letter home after being discharged from here. At home, find a secluded spot. Dig a grave, put this letter inside it, and burn it. When it's all burnt, perform proper burial rites for your father and cover the grave with soil. Then walk away without looking back.'

After seven days in the loony bin, I was released and given thirty days to recuperate at home. I performed the burial rites for my father as a first order of business upon arrival at my humble abode. After the funeral, no tears were shed. It was the most liberating moment of my life. I felt at ease and I knew, from that moment, that I was on my way to a full recovery. You now understand my lack of feeling regarding my father's death. He had to die in order for me to live.

1

Dark secret revealed: I was molested as a child

I hold a dark family secret. I was molested as a child. To this day, I am a wounded adult male. At the time of the evil deed, I was too young to comprehend the magnitude of this sexual assault. However, as a pre-programmed heterosexual male, I intuitively knew that male genitals shouldn't be used in furtherance of sexual pleasure with another male.

Since 2016, my mind has been fixed on this dark chapter of my life. The more I think about it, the more dirty, uncared for, vulnerable and worthless I feel. I am in a perpetual emotional pain. I am heavy-hearted.

This is the first time I am able to disclose this dastardly deed. It has taken me over thirty years to speak out. Yes, it has always been on my mind, but every time it came to full consciousness, I pushed the problem down into the dim recesses of my mind.

The attack happened intermittently over a period of a month. It took me a long time to fully realise what was happening.

Here is the genesis of the story. When my younger sister was born, my mother decided that I was old enough to join my brothers in their separate hut. I was not happy about my mother's decision. I knew I would miss the warmth and comfort of sleeping next to her. I always felt relaxed next to my mom. She was truly my protector and first love. Grudgingly, I relented a week after she had issued the instruction.

It would be a white lie to say I looked forward to this relocation. It felt like my whole being was being uprooted. All I knew, the warmth and comfort, were left behind. I craved the reassurance of knowing that my mom was next to me, to love and protect me. Obviously, on my first night, I struggled to sleep. I had a severe fear of the dark. Psychologists claim that it is a common fear in children and, to a varying degree, in adults. But my fear was not of the darkness itself, but of the possible or imagined dangers it concealed. Voices in my head kept telling me that an intruder was going to break in at any moment to steal young boys like me. I was petrified of going to sleep without the reassurance of my mom: 'I am here for you, my boy. You're safe. God loves you. Don't listen to the voices in your head.'

Under the new arrangement, I was suddenly upgraded to sleeping in a formal bed. Yes, I used to sleep on the floor with my mom and other siblings. But there was a catch: I had to share the bed with my middle brother. On my first night, there was some excitement about finally being able to sleep in a bed. But what little excitement I felt was short-lived.

On subsequent nights of sharing the bed with my middle brother, I started feeling uncomfortable. At first, I thought it was all in my mind, but the feeling of discomfort continued relentlessly.

I had to use my tiny brain to get to the bottom of my discomfort. I made a plan to stay awake after lights-out so I could fully investigate the thing that was bothering me. On previous occasions, the thing that had made me uncomfortable was something akin to human flesh rubbing against my thighs and a bodily movement that had a domino effect on the bed as a whole. It was very strange. I didn't report this new phenomenon to my mother or my middle brother.

I had a theory, though. My theory was that my middle brother was rubbing his penis against my thighs to amuse himself sexually. As I said, I was – and remain – pre-programmed as a heterosexual male. At that point, I already had my first crush, on a classmate named Zodwa. I wasn't sure what it meant, exactly, to have a girl-friend or to have sex. But my intuition was that it was something to behold.

On the day of my formal investigation into the rubbing sensation against my thighs, I went to sleep as usual, except that I wasn't asleep at all. It wasn't long after lights-out that the movement began. Lo and behold! It was my middle brother causing the bed to move. His genitals were pressed against my young thighs. I kept still. Towards the end of the movement, he groaned and moaned, and then I felt a watery substance on my thighs. I was stunned, paralysed to the core. Yet he acted as if nothing had happened: minutes later, he rolled over and went to sleep. My worst fear was confirmed: I had been sexually violated for a month. Recalling this episode terrifies me to this day.

The next day, I asked my mother for a floor mat. She acceded to my request without asking any questions. From that day onwards, I slept on the floor. There was no movement on the floor mat, nothing rubbing against my thighs. I had some peaceful sleep, at least, although I was always on the lookout in case he joined me on the floor mat. I never confronted him. I never reported this episode to my mother or to any other person until I told my wife in 2017.

Despite the passage of time, I haven't healed. I won't forgive. I loathe my brother. I wish he were dead. This is a natural feeling. In *Toxic Parents*, her seminal work on toxic relationships, psychologist

Dr Susan Forward says you don't have to forgive your tormentors. 'If I forgive you, we can pretend that what happened wasn't so terrible,' she writes. I am ready to confront my demons, even if it means breaking the feudal family peace.

2

Mixing bodies and cultures: Love, race and prejudice

When it comes to marriage, I jumped off the cliff: I married a white woman. As we know, interracial intimate relationships continue to be fraught with controversy, despite our post-apartheid, world-renowned, liberal Constitution that guarantees equal rights and forbids racism. In our seventeen years of courtship and marriage, our interracial intimate relationship has been no exception.

For the purposes of this book, I refer to my white wife only as the proverbial English wife – or, more appropriately, as Professor D. Not only did I marry an Englishwoman, I also married above my intellectual station. When our courtship began, she was a PhD candidate at the University of the Witwatersrand and a senior lecturer at what was then the University of Natal. At the time, I was a mature student still only doing my undergraduate studies in journalism. Later, she inspired me to pursue my postgraduate studies. In essence, I crossed both the race and class divide in one fell swoop.

I must admit that my wife hates being referred to as a white woman. She sees herself as just a woman. I see her as my partner – nothing more, and nothing less. Of course, it doesn't help that she listens to Miriam Makeba, and has a collection of music by the finest black South African jazz musicians, including the late Sipho Gumede and Zim Ngqawana. There is definitely nothing white about dancing to the sweet melodies of the late singer, songwriter and live-performance maestro Busi Mhlongo.

In the early days of our courtship, I often asked myself about the extent of her whiteness. If there are special behavioural traits inherent in being white, well, she showed none. To make matters worse, she had been a fervent anti-apartheid activist and a card-carrying member of the ANC since its unbanning. Is she on a trip to be black? Am I on the road to whiteness?

As for me, the onset of my romantic involvement with Professor D. came as no surprise. In truth, I had imagined myself marrying across the colour line eight years before I met my wife. There was nothing melodramatic or political about my imaginations. I was entangled in an emotional fantasy love affair with a white Afrikaans woman named Ria. At the time, Ria was the closest a white girl had ever come to treating me like – well, a human being. To talking to me, and being my friend and comrade. Secretly, I was in love with her. The chemistry I felt for Ria was pure and unemotional, yet it cut deep into my soul. We weren't dating, but our friendship planted the idea that black and white could, in fact, love each other and be together.

In marrying a white woman, I crossed the colour line consciously and, in the process, mixed bodies and cultures. As a result, I came face to face with racial prejudice and racial discrimination. Scholars of interracial intimate relationships and marriages have observed that '[n]egative attitudes toward interracial unions … provide for formidable psychological and emotional barriers to interracial contact, helping to maintain a racially stratified society'.

'This is the biggest mistake you have ever made,' said my English wife's best friend of many years. Being referred to as 'the biggest mistake' still hurts as much today as it did then. When my then girlfriend reported those words to me, I felt the full weight of apartheid discrimination that determined whom to love, marry and have sex with. It is not the only example of direct racial hatred I experienced in the seventeen years of our relationship. Yet this particular incident continues to fester like a sore. I knew the racial offender on a first-name basis. I had – erroneously – somewhat respected her. I thought of her, at the very least, as a liberal and enlightened whitey. I was wrong. This despite the fact that my relationship with my English wife began years after the removal from our statutes of the three laws that had made interracial intimate relationships a criminal offence: the Prohibition of Mixed Marriages Act, 1949 (repealed in 1985), the Immorality Amendment Act, 1957 (repealed in 1986) and the Group Areas Act, 1950 (repealed in 1990). Yet, in post-apartheid South Africa, she still found fraternising across racial lines offensive. Conversely, we found it liberating and life-affirming.

Unfortunately, she wasn't a lone wolf; my own people (read: blacks) had a mouthful to say. I am a traitor; I will increase through birth another race, different from mine – coloureds. So the line went. It is argued that opposition to interracial intimate relationships may indicate what Ratele, whom Claire Lisa Jaynes quotes in her MA thesis, has named 'subtle racism'. At its core, this new form of racism is no less racist or offensive than 'old-fashioned' racism; it is just disguised in a more 'sophisticated' and socially accepted argument, that of opposing intimate relationships between people classified as belonging to different racial groups. Justifications for this opposition are based on supposedly non-racist reasons, such as concern for the welfare of the children produced by such relationships, as Jaynes quotes in her thesis.

The hurtful word 'coloured' pierces my heart every day. Strangely, it comes from friends, foes and strangers alike. Most of these comments about breeding another race originate from black people. In their racial thinking, I have committed the ultimate crime, a crime of passion across the colour line. I am effectively sleeping with the enemy, they claim. It is a pedantic detail that this event occurred deep into post-apartheid South Africa. I even lost a close friend who, unbeknown to me, was entangled in a fantasy love affair with me. She didn't hold back: 'I can't be friends with you now that you're dating a white woman. I simply can't go on and be with you while you're dating whites.' I was stunned: I had no idea that, firstly, she was a racist and, secondly, that she was emotionally invested in our friendship.

Sadly, not even Durban – where we lived at the time – was ready for an interracial couple walking the streets, chatting, kissing and holding hands with gay abandon. Many a time, we elicited hostile stares and outright prejudice. I recall us walking into a restaurant once, holding hands, and sitting ourselves down. Seconds, then minutes, passed. Nobody brought us menus. Nobody took our drinks order. Nobody bothered to tell us we were not welcome. We had to figure it out for ourselves that we had touched a raw nerve of whiteness and its bedfellows, prejudice and naked racism. We walked out and never set foot in that establishment again. Thankfully, that restaurant didn't last long.

Luckily, a sizeable number of my comrades saw nothing wrong with me dating a white woman. They saw only a picture of the new South Africa: the Rainbow Nation. When I first realised that I had fallen in love with Professor D., I sought political counsel from one of my closest comrades. Without a second thought, he said, 'If you love her, go for it.'

I am glad that new empirical research proves that interracial intimate relationships are no longer a novelty. A 2011 study on interracial marriages, conducted by Acheampong Yaw Amoateng, a research professor of sociology and family studies at North-West University in Mafikeng, provided good news about race relations in South Africa. Researchers examined the likelihood of South Africans marrying outside of their race, as well as the factors influencing interracial marriages. The study showed that, in 1996, the chance of someone marrying outside his or her race was 303:1. In 2011, this likelihood had increased to 95:1. While marrying within one's race is still the norm in South Africa, studies show that this is slowly starting to change. And groups who have previously been found least likely to marry outside their race – Asians, Indians and whites – are increasingly choosing partners of another race. A recorded 5 per cent of coloureds, Asians and Indians chose interracial marriage, while whites are the least likely among all races to do so. The most common interracial marriage is that between blacks and coloureds. Black men are the most likely to marry outside of their race, while black women are least likely to enter into an interracial marriage.

However, interracial intimate relationships aren't always smooth sailing. Although they are now legal, they are still a highly controversial topic. Attitudes towards interracial marriages and intimate relationships in South Africa may represent some kind of yardstick by which to measure the degree of transition the country has achieved thus far, writes Jaynes in her thesis. In my case, the issue of cultural differences runs too deep. I am Zulu by birth; she is English. I am a carnivore; she is a vegetarian. I believe in sorceresses and ancestors; she doesn't. She is a non-practising Catholic; I am a non-practising believer in uMvelinqangi, the African God of Creation. These differences have far-reaching consequences.

For instance, to appease my parents after our wedding, I suggested a traditional wedding at which we would slaughter a cow to introduce the new bride to the ancestors. My wife does not believe in animal slaughter on principle. Obviously, she doesn't want to be associated with the willy-nilly slaughter of animals in her name. She refused. The stalemate continues; my parents continue to push for the traditional wedding, in vain. I have decided to choose my wife over my parents.

Despite this traditional-wedding hiatus, my family has long accepted my white wife. My mother speaks only words of kindness about her. She is regarded as an important member of the Mncube family. I am also fortunate that my English wife's family have also accepted me and my Zuluness. In an interview for this book, my mother-in-law said:

'So much joy from watching the two of you grow and mature together. It needed a strong love bond to make a success of a mixed-race marriage, and you can be proud. Be proud, also, of your daughter – she is a special product of two very special parents. So, my dear son-in-law, who likes to call himself a young Zulu boy but who is, in fact, a mature Zulu man with a lovely sense of humour and a kind and generous heart, continue looking after your wife and daughter, continue enjoying life. We wish you the success that you deserve.'

Despite this warm reception, the question lingers: Have I forsaken my belief in my Zulu ancestors? The short answer is no. I happily call myself a Zulu cultural delinquent and a part-time darkie.

On the bright side, love lives in my house. Every day, I wake up to the most beautiful woman on earth. She is blessed with a voice that mellows like evening's purple dome and her face, when she smiles, has those cute dimples. She is a plus-sized woman of medium height and fair complexion. I call her my original yellow-bone. The most important part is, of course, her character and inner beauty. She is imbued with an abundance of kindness, and she has a heart of gold.

Thirteen years ago, we were blessed with a beautiful daughter, Miss N. Two years ago, she told me that she had resolved the issue of her racial identity: 'Dad, I am a suburban Zulu girl.' She will have nothing to do with the apartheid-inspired political identity that mixed-race South Africans are considered to be coloureds. It is therefore my contention that we need to re-imagine the tired concepts of apartheid-fuelled race identity and racial profiling. We are human beings before the socially constructed notion of race. Let us love and let us live.

I concur with Claire Lisa Jaynes's conclusion in her MA thesis 'Interracial Intimate Relationships in Post-apartheid South Africa', that '[i]t is only within the ideology of racism that people have "colour"'.

3

Whiteness and I

In a 2016 column published in *The Mercury* newspaper, social activist Justin Foxton further obfuscated the debate about whiteness and the privilege that goes with it. Foxton wrote: '... thinking about my own identity ... caused me to reflect on the fact that, whilst I am a white South African, I would currently rather not be'.

Foxton clearly doesn't get it; whilst I am black South African, I would rather not be. I have always found my blackness disabling. The burden of black bodies is too much to bear. Today, I confess to being one of those who have had an ambivalent attitude to race and racial identity. Yes, I am black. I look and speak like them, but I don't have black feelings any more. I am in a perpetual nostalgic mode akin to 1994 rainbowism. Interestingly, my ambivalence about my blackness dates back to the early 1980s.

I look at the world through the prism of natives and whites living side by side in a state of nirvana, except that I am no longer a native. I refuse to let go of this dream. I do not feel the same black pain as that of the Stellenbosch student protester who yelled at Western Cape premier Helen Zille on live television, saying, 'I've worked to get here! It is not a privilege to be here!' The protester added that her mother, who had worked as a domestic worker for the past fifteen years, made R2 400 a month. 'Where are the labour laws in this land?' she asked Zille.

I can't comprehend her pain, as my mother was never a domestic worker and my father never worked as a gardener for a white family. I have never worked in white suburbia either, doing gardening jobs like some black boys did in my neighbourhood.

Instead, my parents grew up on white farms as labour tenants. They have fond memories of serving Afrikaner farmers during their labour tenancy in Vryheid. The only regret they still have is the manner in which they were expelled, allegedly for defiance. After a scuffle with the farmer, they were exiled to the northern part of the erstwhile KwaZulu homeland and settled at Eshowe. To this day, they hanker for the good old days on the farms, where apparently food was in abundance. Strange fellows, you may think.

As the adage goes, the apple did not fall far from the tree: I have my own 'native nostalgia'. It began in the early 1980s, long before I knew about the now-immortalised Nelson Mandela's statement at the opening of his defence during the Rivonia Trial, on 20 April 1964, when he told the presiding judge: 'I have cherished the ideal of a democratic and free society in which all persons live together in harmony and with equal opportunities.'

I have vivid memories of my father breaking bread with a white man in our humble homestead in the rolling hills of Eshowe. While my father and his white farmer friend were busy sipping tea, the country was in flames due to popular resistance and violent township protests – which led to apartheid Prime Minister P.W. Botha declaring a state of emergency. Throughout the popular uprising against apartheid, my father maintained cordial relations with many white males. In fact, when word was out on the streets that the KwaZulu Legislative Assembly was looking for someone with the rare skills of building traditional Zulu huts and a deep knowledge of Zulu history, my father was the sole contender. He was recommended for the job by his white farmer friend. That's how it came to pass that my father became the Chief Induna during the restoration of King Cetshwayo kaMpande's Ondini palace.

The sight of my father sipping tea with a white farmer convinced me that whiteness was the way to go. I said to myself: When I grow up, I want to be like a white man. The white farmer drove a Land Rover. He wore proper clothes. He had a farm. Most importantly, he had people working for him. But my fantasy to be like a white man was temporarily shelved when I became aware of the word 'apartheid'. I became extremely angry with white men in general, but remained indifferent to my father's white friend. My anger didn't last long. By 1986, when I joined the anti-apartheid forces led by the ANC Mission in Exile, the comrades in the underground explained to me that it was not about white men, but the system of apartheid. That was my saving grace: my dream of being white was reignited.

It is no surprise, then, that the book *Cry, the Beloved Country* by Alan Paton – a white liberal – set the tone for my political activism more than any other book or political education class.

Fast-forward to my arrival, in 1993, as a greenhorn in the city of Durban for tertiary education. This was a game-changer. I became immersed in ANC politics dominated by *them* – white people, with an overwhelming number of white girls and a mixture of white male conscription resisters, underground activists and academics. I fell in love with white girls at first sight. I began to fantasise about having a white girlfriend. I had never experienced the chemistry that existed between me and white girls with black girls. This insatiable desire for white girls eventually had a happy ending – I am married to one of them, a one-time ANC activist.

In reality, I have always struggled to come to terms with my blackness. I find it heavy going. But the straw that broke the camel's back was when, on three occasions, totalling four years, I stayed in black townships around Durban. Never before had I felt such total alienation. I must admit I've always found comfort in white suburbia, and I think my whiteness is now complete.

On 27 September 2015, something of epic proportions happened. I knew it was coming. It started slowly. I guess I had to be eased into it. Finally, I dreamt in English. As they say, if you can swear in it and dream in it, it's your mother tongue. So, folks, finally I am *uNgamla* – the equivalent of a white man.

In conclusion, as seasoned author Njabulo Ndebele once said, I am bothered by the phenomenon of a black majority in power seeming to reduce itself to the status of complainants, as if they had a limited capacity to do anything more significant about the situation at hand than drawing attention to it. The recent spectacle of the #FeesMustFall movement brought to bear the burden of black bodies in our society. How does one explain that black students, clad in ANC regalia, stormed the ANC headquarters, Luthuli House, and the Union Buildings? My greatest challenge is to explain to my daughter what it means to be coloured, rather than to be bothered with the burden of blackness.

READERS' RESPONSES

Fred Khumalo: Dream on, brother. It's good to dream. But you are Bhekisisa, a black South African. You were defined at birth. Perhaps in some utopia or nirvana where race never mattered, we wouldn't be talking about it. You father did what he did in order to survive. Big up to him. But to wake up, just because you 'dreamt in English' and decide you are no longer black is downright silly. Ridiculous.

Yes, you embrace the identity that you choose to, but your circumstances will always remind you who you are, where you live. This is South Africa, my friend. It's no accident that the majority are black and poor, and that you will drive to the four corners of our beautiful country and never come across a squatter camp or a township for whites. Squatter camps, as you know, are the by-products of a system that classified us racially. And, in this country, race has always been a class determinant. Don't tell me about a pocketful of BEE types and some members of the black middle class. Very minuscule and insignificant.

Anyway, you've chosen your path. And it is your journey. Are these protests rekindling the embers of guilt or some indefinable regret? No, you don't have to feel guilty about how you want to define yourself, or how you would like others to perceive you. It's your life; it's your choice. But the gurgling brooks of this land, our beautiful land, and the laughing sparrows, and the mountains with their frowning faces, will always remind you who you are. These will always force you to take a dose of reality. Embracing a new consciousness, an all-embracing philosophy, does not mean you have to jettison that which is you. You can't negate your true essence. What the hell is that? Wake up and smell the *umqombothi*, bra. Nat Nakasa used to think he wasn't a black man ... until he went to America. The rest is history.

SSK Khumallo: Very brave to pen such a letter, given the ruthless race police out there. Good for you, man.

Sue Alcock: You're a courageous and honest man, Bheks. Introspection has never frightened you. It's one of your finest qualities.

Angela Abrahams: Your honest reflection is going to have many of us thinking, reflecting and talking for days. That is what writing is about Bhekisisa Mncube. Load your response already ...

4

Meeting my white in-laws for the first time

I had the misfortune of meeting my white in-laws for the first time in the first year I was courting my new girlfriend, now the proverbial English wife. Yes, I know – it sounds like speed dating. But it is not what you think.

In our second month of dating, I was literally going to be homeless. I had just completed my undergraduate studies, which meant that my prestigious international scholarship had come to an abrupt end. I had not secured an internship, which would have given me some form of an income. In reality, I was penniless and homeless. So, my new love offered to let me move in with her temporarily until I sorted myself out. I agreed. I moved straight from the Durban University of Technology residence, known as Corlo Court, into her apartment at the end of June 2001, and never left. It was par for the course that, one way or another, I would bump into members of her family. I must say, the move itself was seamless, but culture shock awaited me. I did not have the cultural capital to navigate this uncharted territory. I was a novice in the true sense of the word: sadly, I hadn't even begun to imagine the scope and magnitude of the evolution that was set to unfold until it hit me right in the face.

The apartment was an immaculate one-bedroom with a modern

kitchen and formal study. The study was a treasure trove filled with exciting books. The apartment also boasted a small but beautiful garden. I had to store my meagre clothing possessions in the same wardrobe as my girlfriend. My kitchen paraphernalia (including pots, spoons and plates) was relegated to the unused former servants' quarters. It was only years later that my inadequate kitchen utensils were donated to the Durban Highway Hospice. Clearly, they had no use in my new environment – possibly, the fear was that they would quickly cause the apartment's kitchen to depreciate in value.

I had never in my life been a live-in lover. I had never even slept in another man's house, let alone a woman's (shacks excluded). I wondered aloud as to the meaning of my newly acquired status. Was I a tenant with benefits? Overnight, I became a de facto boss to two people (by far older than me): the gardener and the housekeeper.

And I had to share a space (read: bed) with my new girlfriend every day. I was terrified. The longest I had ever shared a bedroom with a woman was a maximum of weekends and, in the case of Lindiwe, five days.

Day one. First thing in the morning, my love was in the kitchen. She fiddled with some machine and suddenly she had black coffee in her mug. She drank that black coffee thingy without even adding a teaspoon of sugar. I was horrified. She had a machine just to make black coffee? I had brought some of my favourite coffee with me. You guessed it: Nescafé Ricoffy. I considered Nescafé Ricoffy with Cremora milk powder to be the Rolls-Royce of coffees; I was wrong. It wasn't long before my love introduced me to Ethiopian coffee beans and the pleasure of drinking hot, and black, coffee. To this day, I take my coffee-drinking very seriously – it has to be a double-shot black Americano. The bean must have been sourced somewhere in Africa or Colombia. Talk about cultural assimilation. In fact, today in my house we don't even buy coffee any more. We buy the beans. Not only do we have a sophisticated coffee machine, but we also have a coffee grinder. And I no longer add sugar to my coffee. People who talk about the contested and non-scientific terms 'white monopoly capital' and 'state capture' have nothing on me. I am truly and honestly captured.

The second quandary was, of course, eating habits. My girlfriend had told me that she was a vegetarian. I had, up to that point, never touched a vegetarian, never mind lived with one. She quickly learnt to make chicken dishes, as I did; I still just love my chicken. So, day one ended with two separate cooking pots – one a vegetarian dish and the other a chicken stew. I watched the whole cooking session in awe. She had *real* spices – not the run-of-the-mill stuff you buy from giant supermarkets, but spices from specialist shops. Every dish she cooked came from a recipe. And she routinely bought cook books and magazines. This was all new to me. We had a formal breakfast and a proper dinner every day. From whence I came, you ate fast food at irregular times.

It dawned on me, that very day, that this new venture was fraught with peril. I couldn't imagine it being sustainable. Again, I was wrong. To this day, my English wife prepares yummy meals – yes, from recipe books, which have grown in number over the past seventeen years.

The third complication was that I was no longer free. At least, that was how I felt. I had to report to someone about my whereabouts. To make matters worse, we were living deep in the historically white suburb of Glenwood, Durban. At the time, it had virtually no public transport, except the municipal buses known as Mynah buses. I learnt much later that there was, indeed, public transport in the form of minibus taxis, but these operated in the mornings and afternoons to cater mostly for domestic workers. I had no car. I was as poor as a church mouse. This meant that I was apartment-bound unless, of course, we were together, driving somewhere. When I was in the apartment alone, I felt lost and isolated.

For starters, the whole neighbourhood was too quiet for my liking. The only sounds were those of birds and an occasional car driving past. All my life I had lived in vibrant (read: noisy) places. To this day, I find it hard to report on my whereabouts. On the bright side, today I swear by the historically white suburbs. For the life of me, I can't imagine how people live a quality life in townships and informal settlements with all that noise, pollution and commotion, especially the unregulated twenty-four-hour shebeens and taverns.

The saving grace of our young love became our mutual love for books, jazz and politics. Our vibrant social life included attending literary events and jazz performances, and visiting book stores and art galleries. I learnt early in our courtship that my new white girl-friend had an alter ego. And, she was an artist of note. As a testimony to her artistic prowess, her art hangs in our house to this day. I was tagging along to all these social rendezvous with a combination of glee and gloom. I missed my carefree lifestyle that had no programme other than studying, reading and smoking. In between, there were wild parties on campus, and clubs and societies that occupied one's life. I had never been ready to fit into a routine. I am still not.

The only real snag was that, as part of our energetic social life, we had too many dinners at friends' houses. At these dinners, I always found myself as the only darkie, standing out like a sore thumb. For the most part, it felt like I was nothing more than a subject in an anthropological study. There was an unhealthy interest in me and my miserable life. I constantly had to explain who I was and, of course, how I had met my white girlfriend. The whole thingy was clearly a novelty for all of us. Compounding the who-are-you moment was that, at the time, my curriculum vitae was so thin you could see through its pages.

The most challenging aspect of the dinners, however, was the humble bottle of wine. Yes, my girlfriend's friends drank mostly wine, and occasionally gin and tonic. I was no wine drinker. Yet few of the friends made beer provisions for me at these dinners. My worst experience was when the friends assumed I knew how to open a wine bottle. Truth is, I didn't know where to start. More often than not, my girlfriend saved me from imminent embarrassment.

I never felt like an equal partner at all these dinners. There was a sense of loneliness, a loss of something intangible: my blackness; yes, the same blackness that disables me. As Bafana Khumalo once quipped, 'I was feeling very black. In fact, I was so black at that moment, you couldn't see me in the dark. Steve Biko and his Black Consciousness Movement had nothing on me.'

All these hurdles did nothing to prepare me for the meeting with my very first white brother-in-law: a cousin who shall remain nameless. Hardly ten minutes into our conversation in his house, he laid into me, asking how much I was contributing to the household budget. The third degree he gave me fitted in with the racism discourse in the realm of whiteness. Whites were constructed as rich, the 'haves', contrasted with the black 'have-nots'. It was clear that he didn't buy the story of a blossoming love affair between a black Zulu boy and a white girl. He clearly surmised that this was just nothing more than a financial transaction, and that I was on a mission: political Armageddon and pushing the payback agenda. Talk about white privilege. It felt like a kangaroo court. Clearly, my motive was

41

suspicious, so I had to be ambushed. I had no ready-made answers. Fact is, I was contributing nothing because I had nothing.

But my dearest cousin is not a lone wolf in misunderstanding the whiteness/blackness nexus. In 'Interracial Intimate Relationships in Post-apartheid South Africa', Claire Lisa Jaynes makes an interesting observation from her interviews: that whites are depicted as materialistic. It was said in these interviews that, in order for a black person to attract a white mate, you needed to have money and a car. This precondition of interracial relationships is also said to apply to friendships ('if I have it [money] then that will be easier for me to be friends'). I didn't fit in with the dangerous delusion fuelled by nothing other than a racial stereotype. Yes, I was dating a white woman, despite the fact that I had had an inferior education. I remained black and poor. My poverty was visible, because I had no car or money.

Luckily, my situation changed quickly. In July of that same year, I started freelancing for the *Sunday World* newspaper and later secured an office job as a communications trainee at a non-governmental organisation, known at the time as the Centre for Public Participation (CPP). Suddenly, I was attending sittings of the KwaZulu-Natal Provincial Legislature and portfolio committee meetings as a parliamentary monitor, and gave interviews on radio. My stature entered an upward trajectory. By the time the white father- and mother-in-law jetted into South Africa from France, I was ready for any eventuality. My white parents-in-law were renowned hoteliers in a small village in France. They came to South Africa every year to spend summer here, as they had no clientele in France during the winter months.

For some reason, my girlfriend found it necessary to report to her parents, before they landed in South Africa, that she had met someone. For the longest time, I wasn't sure whether she had made the disclosure: He is black. Interviewed for this book, my mother-in-law reveals: 'We were living overseas when that tentative phone call came from my daughter, announcing that she had met a man she liked very much and that his name was Bheki.' After this telling telephone conversation between mother and daughter, I was suddenly told that I must prepare myself to meet the parents upon their arrival in South Africa. We had been invited to dinner.

In preparation, I inquired about the family dynamics. I was told to relax ('My parents are my parents …'), but I learnt that my mother-in-law was English – born, bred and raised in Durban. She comes from the rich history of the Clarks of Clark Road, who owned land in Glenwood. To this day, there is a Clark Road in the city. My father-in-law is a Mauritian who arrived in South Africa at the age of ten. He came from a poor background. Yet he pulled himself up by his bootstraps to become one of the successful men in his family. He valued reading and education in general, so he educated all his children up to tertiary level.

We arrived in tow at the preferred restaurant. The elderly couple stood up and hugged and kissed their daughter. I stood behind her, watching the spectacle of kisses on each cheek. I had never seen such a kissing extravaganza before. The moment passed too quickly – before I could even blink, it was my turn to be greeted. I didn't know whether to offer my cheeks for a kiss, or a good old-fashioned Zulu handshake. It seemed that they sensed my unease, as they both settled for a weak English handshake. I was relieved.

We sat down and, you guessed right, I was asked which wine I preferred. I had practised my line, which went something like this: 'I will have dry white, please, if anyone else is having the same.' I had done my homework. The trick worked. I sounded educated and sophisticated. We then settled down to a most mundane chat, as if we had known one another for years. The chat progressed organically. There was no question-and-answer session designed only for me. I didn't feel pressurised by a barrage of questions. The night progressed quickly, without a hitch. We ordered mains while the amber liquids flowed freely. I left the dinner table reassured that my new white parents-in-law had no qualms about me dating their daughter. At the very least, they had accepted what they couldn't change. It was clear that there was going to be no interference on their part. After dinner, I told my girlfriend, 'I love your parents.'

However, occasionally during the dinner, my father-in-law would go off on a tangent with his dry sense of humour. He asked jokingly whether I was prepared to pay *lobola* (dowry) for his daughter, insisting that she preferred live cows. We all laughed, but the joke did not go down well with my mother-in-law, who proceeded to chastise her husband. You see, my mother-in-law is an adherent of good, old-fashioned English manners. There is table talk, and then there are bad jokes that may offend sensitive listeners. Over the years, I have watched her keep things on the straight and narrow.

On the other hand, my father-in-law is a free-spirited, quick-witted maverick. He has quite a sharp tongue. One can't be unnerved by what he says, or the way he says it. In his world, there are no holy cows. He will tell you how stupid the Afrikaner nationalist was, then move on organically to deal a deadly blow to the ANC for dilly-dallying on important matters such as labour law. Given half a chance, he would lecture you on French politics and never hide his distaste for France's rigid labour regime that killed, rather than opened up, job opportunities. Reassuringly, I have learnt that he is, in fact, an honest and loving family man.

Over the years, they have continued to shower my side of the family with love and support. My mother-in-law is in awe of our staying power.

In 2017, my father-in-law turned eighty. In my wife's speech, she retold a famous story about her father during the apartheid era, when he was rumoured to have been a member of the South African Communist Party. The story, I am told, caused consternation in some quarters, yet he could not have cared less. Apparently, he'd told anyone who cared to listen that he did not support the National Party regime. In my telephone message to wish him a happy birthday, I used the honorific Mr. He quickly chastised me, preferring me to use his first name instead.

5

'Mom, meet my white girlfriend'

It was a historical improbability that my new white girlfriend would be introduced to my family. For three long years, I kept my family in the dark and fed them on manure, like mushrooms, until our daughter was born in 2004. Suddenly, the matter of the official introduction became rather a necessity. My younger sister had known about my liaison with my white girlfriend from the beginning and had decided against spilling the beans. I have no clue about her reasons; I had not asked her to draw a veil of secrecy.

In reality, I had had many girlfriends, and none of them were lucky enough to be introduced to my family. As far as my family was concerned, I may have remained a virgin well into my thirties. I always found the girlfriend introduction thingy quite daunting. I had tried to avoid it like the plague. So, to prepare for my maiden girlfriend introduction, I phoned my mom and explained that I was bringing her a potential bride (*makoti*). For the whole conversation, I was in a state of panic: I was finally going to break new ground. Yet my mom was over the moon. I edited out all finer details, such as that she was white and that we had already had a child. I was a nervous wreck. I had never been on this journey before.

Apparently, introducing your significant other to your family is a big deal. It sends a message that your relationship is serious. And it may mean that the relationship is due, and ready for, an upgrade. According to the *Gentleman's Journal*, this 'meeting' will be more terrifying for you than anything you have ever dealt with in the boardroom: worse than the day you had to make your personal assistant redundant, or when the stock exchange plummeted and you found yourself in a pool of piranhas, asking you to save the entire company. 'Quite frankly, gentlemen, this will test you more than anything you have ever done before,' the *Journal* writes.

It *did* test my resolve. A million questions raced through my head. What if someone in the family found our dalliance offensive and couldn't hide it? I even imagined my father going off on a tangent, cursing me all over again. Confounding the problem was that I hadn't made up my mind about the future with my then girlfriend. I was living in the moment and it felt good. In my mind, she had to spend at least six years as my girlfriend before there could be any talk of an upgrade. Yes, six years, because my only other long-term relationship had died at five. I wasn't convinced that any of my relationships would last longer than that. If one did, it meant (so I reasoned) that we were meant to be together. But, I digress.

The moment of truth arrived sooner than we imagined. I had prepared my girlfriend for the worst. In my briefing, I told her that my family were very conservative Zulus who swear by the ancestors. I told her that they believed in animal slaughter at the slightest provocation to appease the ancestors. I made it clear that if they decided to slaughter an animal to welcome her, I couldn't stop them. As you know, my girlfriend has always been averse to killing animals. I disclosed that, politically speaking, we were also at odds, as both my parents belong to the Inkatha Freedom Party. I warned her that my father had threatened to disown us as youngsters if we voted for the ANC.

Now, this titbit about politics was important, as we were both enthusiastic ANC members. I also made it known that I was not quite my father's favourite son – that we had fallen out in 1993, when I refused to join the police department of the KwaZulu Bantustan government. My father had walked out of his own house after I made it clear that I was headed for Durban to further my tertiary studies. Besides, we had been further estranged since 2006, when my psychologist asked me to 'kill' my father to overcome my depression, the malady of the Mncube family. So, I considered myself fatherless. Again, I digress.

Anyway, as a form of insurance, I asked my younger sister to be present at the official white-girlfriend introduction. At least my girlfriend would see a familiar face and have someone to converse with in English. Not only is my girlfriend white, but she speaks no Zulu. This language barrier was huge in that, as a new daughter-in-law, one must make a lasting first impression. How on earth do you make an impression if you can't *khuluma* (talk)? At least I didn't have to worry about her speaking out of turn.

I wasn't sure how my family would react to seeing a white daughter-in-law. I didn't know how to prepare them for this eventuality, so I sprang a surprise on them.

In the penultimate stages of our preparations, we had to resolve the issue of the dress code. My father forbids women from wearing pants. In any event, my family tradition dictates that a daughter-in-law has to cover up, including wearing a *doek*. So I bought her a stylish, Xhosa-inspired dress that covered everything, as my parents preferred, but she refused to wear a *doek* to cover her hair.

We arrived, as planned, on a Saturday afternoon. We alighted from the car, a familiar-looking woman emerging, holding a baby. Surprise number one: she was white. Surprise number two: she was known to my family as an academic who had taught my late brother. She had, on two occasions, seen both my parents in the flesh – at my brother's funeral, and at the awarding of his posthumous honours degree. Surprise number three: there was a baby. My daughter was six weeks old at the time.

We started to approach the family homestead, my mother and other family members standing outside one of the huts to welcome us. From my vantage point, I could discern a sense of both disbelief and sheer wonder. But there was still tension in the air – unsurprising, given the magnitude of the occasion. My mother blurted out words of joy. She ululated, sang and danced, as she is wont to do when exciting events occur. But she was the only happy chappy in the whole group. She even managed to hold our daughter in her arms; in the picture, though, it looks like she is in a precarious position. To this day, my daughter complains that my mother was holding her like a pocket of potatoes.

My father stood there motionless, looking perplexed. My other siblings still had to process the atmosphere, so their faces were expressionless. This was new to all of us. I had brought a white woman into a black Zulu family. I am told my grandparents had had run-ins with white people during colonial times. Possibly, some ancestors had died believing that white people were their enemies. Who could blame them? But, she is here now – holding out the hand of friendship and saying she wants to join this Zulu family. The whole scene resembled a speed session of the Truth and Reconciliation Commission. In a split second, my girlfriend had to make an imaginary confession before my family that she had no apartheid skeletons in her closet so that she could receive an instant pardon.

In retrospect, I think she did receive an instant pardon. There were more words spoken in those silent moments than have been uttered since. As the shock of the moment subsided, we were ushered into the family home.

But not before my father caused a drama to unfold. You see, for many years my father boasted that he spoke better English than the rest of us educated children. We all expected my father to make good on his promise and speak his better English to my white girl-friend. Without any prior discussions, all my siblings were awaiting my father's bombshell. It came; he didn't disappoint. He looked my girlfriend in the eye and said, in some funny language later believed to be Fanakalo (a workplace lingua franca in South Africa for over a hundred years): 'We na thanda lakhaya,' loosely translated to mean: 'You love somebody in this household.' In unison, we burst out laughing until we cried tears of joy. My girlfriend was unperturbed by our laughter as my father continued: 'Mina cela imali khismuzi,' loosely translated as 'May I have money for Christmas.' Although it was early December, my father had the whole Christmas theme running at full speed. We launched into a second frenzy of laughter, and I am sure someone was rolling on the floor.

Our day was made. Most importantly, my father had broken the ice. My girlfriend stood there, grinning from ear to ear. She under-stood nothing and probably wished the whole circus would leave town soon, longing for a moment of silence to reflect on her new journey into the world of the unknown.

Soon thereafter, my mother was on my case. She complained bitterly that I hadn't let them know that I was bringing someone they already knew. She wanted to know why I had kept it a secret for so long. She went on singing the praises of my white girlfriend as if they had grown up together. She couldn't stop telling me how lucky I was to be with her. But she reserved her venom for my sister, who had admitted earlier that she had known about our liaison for three years. She cursed my sister, saying her chest would one day swell with secrets. We all laughed it off. I didn't quite have answers for my mother's barrage of questions. I sensed that she just wanted to get it off her chest, rather than wanting answers. So, I told her to be happy now that she had another granddaughter. Indeed, she was thrilled.

By the time we arrived, cooking had already started. The funny thing is that I had told my family that their new daughter-in-law ate vegetables only. Not only had they met a white woman, but one who eats cheap food, or so the line of thought went. I think they prepared *uphuthu* and beans for her; obviously, there was chicken for the whole family.

While we had prepared mentally, and my family seemed to have reacted positively, we had forgotten to factor in the rest of the community. News spread like wildfire that there was a white girlfriend in the neighbourhood. We were all ill-prepared for the whispers and gossip-mongers. Suddenly, our house became like a shrine. One after the other, neighbours came to see for themselves that there was, indeed, a white *makoti*. It didn't help that my father took me to a group of men who were seated under the big tree at home drinking *umqombothi* and told them, 'This son of mine has a white girlfriend, a real *mlungu* [the colloquial Zulu term for a white person], not painted.' There was a sense of pride and joy in his voice. To him, this was, by any measure, an achievement worth celebrating.

However, the language barrier played havoc with the visitors and potential gossip-mongers. It worked in our favour, as all conversations were understandably kept short and sweet. They would enter the house where we were seated in high spirits, and then

English, *dololo* (slang for not knowing anything or getting nothing). At the time, my girlfriend, in her heavy Durban North English accent, could utter only three Zulu words '*Sawubona. Mina ngiyaphila.*' Loosely translated, this means, 'Hi. I am fine.' Luckily, most conversations ended at the greeting stage, with visitors mumbling something along the lines of, 'Welcome to our neighbourhood.' I utterly refused to play interpreter. This suited us just fine, as we were not prepared for long, drawn-out conversations about nothing.

The weekend went by too fast, and without a hitch. When we waved everyone goodbye and drove off, back to Durban, I felt relief.

The nightmare was over.

6

Four weddings down, three to go

I love my wife. This is not a scientific fact, but an emotional reality. I love her so much that I have already married her four times, and three more wedding ceremonies are still outstanding.

There are two versions of how I met my wife. The first version, possibly more revolutionary, says we met in the ANC underground in the early 1990s. The second version, perhaps closer to the truth, is that we met in 2001, following a brutal attack on my brother Bhekuyise Mncube. Both versions have some elements of truth. Yes, she was an ANC activist and served on the same ANC structures as I did. We attended similar events and shared similar networks, but the truth is we never actually recognised each other in all those encounters. Here is the thing – I was so overwhelmed by white female comrades that my eyes were probably on someone else.

Our second encounter was more dramatic. She came to deliver the news that my brother, who had been missing for three days, was, in fact, dying in a hospital. He had woken up from a coma and remembered the varsity telephone number of his master's degree supervisor – yes, my wife is a nerd. So, that's how she came looking for me at the Durban University of Technology to deliver the news. Unfortunately, my brother didn't make it.

However, something happened the day we were writing my brother's obituary. I was narrating and Professor D. was typing. The more I told her of my brother's story, the more titbits about myself I mentioned. By the time the obituary was completed, we had established that we had, in fact, known each other way back when, in the trenches of the ANC underground. She had edited and designed the only surviving copy of the ANC Umbilo–Glenwood branch newsletter. The main point of the newsletter – apart from spreading propaganda – was to introduce the new members of the branch executive committee, of which I was a part.

After the funeral, I met with her again, to pass on the gratitude of my family for everything she had done for our beloved brother and the bereaved family. This was meant to be our last meeting, but something happened. I recall sitting in her car, completely enchanted by this woman. I was drawn to her dignified beauty, courteous nature and abundance of kindness. It was clear to me that I had to keep talking to her, or my only chance of making something of the moment would be gone in seconds. At some stage, we embraced to say our goodbyes, and then something extraordinary occurred: we kissed. We kissed again, and again. I was so overwhelmed by this historic moment that a tear fell. I knew intuitively then that I was in love. Later that day, we went out for a couple of drinks and parted on good terms. That was the beginning of a whirlwind romance that has lasted seventeen years, and counting. Hardly three months after our first kiss, I moved in with her as a tenant.

Our first wedding was low-key. We were married at the post office. Yes, you can marry someone at the post office without anyone knowing about it. We were both ill-prepared for our first wedding. Our plan was simple – to obtain an affidavit confirming that I was her live-in partner, a requirement for me to be covered by her medical aid. In all honesty, all we needed was an official stamp from a commissioner of oaths. Our commissioner of oaths, clearly a man of some repute, went through the forms and affidavit with a fine-tooth comb. He didn't mince his words: 'Do you guys understand what you're getting yourself into? Are you ready to be married in law?' At first, we chuckled. Then, it hit us: we weren't ready for the legal consequences. We composed ourselves and confirmed that, yes, indeed, we understood the consequences. He stamped the affidavit and signed it; we left as a married couple. We had another good chuckle outside the post office and sealed it with a kiss.

Our second wedding was very serious and formal. We appeared before the Mauritian High Court in Port Louis to swear before a judge that, yes, we knew, indeed, the legal consequences of our marriage. We also had to swear that there was no impediment to our nuptials. We were duly married under both Mauritian and inter-national law.

Our third wedding was more fun, under the open sky at a Mau-ritian beach hotel. The marriage officer explained the rationale thus: 'It is appropriate, therefore, that this wedding of Bhekisisa and Professor D. be under the open sky, where we are close to the earth and to the unity of life, the totality of living things of which we are a part.'

We then did the whole radical thing of making up our own vows: 'I, Bhekisisa, take you, Professor D., as my friend and love, beside me and apart from me, in laughter and in tears, in conflict and tranquillity, asking that you be no other than yourself, loving what I know of you, trusting what I do not know yet, in all the ways that life may find us.' There was no customary 'You may kiss the bride.' Nevertheless, we couldn't escape the kissing part – we kissed in front of a small audience of holidaymakers from all over the world. We then performed another revolutionary act by having our wedding pictures taken alongside the serenity of the Indian Ocean. It was total bliss. No guests. No priest. No fuss. The only official witness was our three-year-old daughter, Miss N; today, she claims to remember nothing of the wedding except that it was too hot and the whole thing was boring.

Our fourth wedding was at our house in Durban, a few weeks after the Mauritian junket. We had invited about fifty guests. It was a jovial event, and amber liquids flowed. We convinced ourselves that we had had enough wedding ceremonies to last us a lifetime. In fact, we erroneously thought that we had gone the whole hog. We were wrong.

Prior to the Mauritian trip, I proudly reported to my family that I was going to get married. I apologised that they couldn't come, due to the exorbitant costs. Upon my return, I duly went home to report the good news in person. My father stunned me. He was furious. He said to my face that I wasn't married.

'When did we kill a cow to ask for a blessing of the ancestors for this so-called marriage? When was *umembeso*?'

In Zulu culture, *umembeso* is when the groom's family takes gifts to the bride's family to thank them for the gift of their new daughter-in-law. The groom's family is welcomed by the father of the bride to the sounds of singing and ululating as one family loses and another gains a daughter. My mother, not to be outdone, politely asked: 'When is the white wedding?'

The snag with the whole Zulu version of the marriage ritual is that it assumes a posture of being a superior culture. According to my parents' narrative, unless I held my wedding as per their template, I was not married. But there is a clash of cultures here. My wife is English. She is the daughter of a French Mauritian father and an English-speaking mother. She was born in Durban. She doesn't believe in white weddings. She refuses to have anything to do with a wedding ceremony involving the willy-nilly killing of poor cows and goats. She has neither a relationship with, nor knowledge of, the whole ancestors thingy. I, too, don't believe in white weddings. And I do not have the financial resources for a fanciful ancestral blessing either.

Nonetheless, I owed my parents and the village of my birth two wedding ceremonies – the traditional, as well as the white, wedding. Oh, we also haven't registered our marriage with our local Home Affairs.

I guess there are three more wedding ceremonies on the horizon.

READERS' RESPONSES

Alfred Mahlangu: I can relate to your gutsy and unconventional story, told with unpretentious simplicity and ideologue-less examination of tradition. Thank you for sharing this heart-warming rendition of how your nuptial contract(s) was sealed ...

Zamo Ndumo: What a beautifully told story – a clash of two cultures! Personally, I would ditch the White Wedding part if I had my way, but knowing our women and this #OPW phenomenon, one would be lucky to get away with what I consider to be an awful waste of money. All the best to you and family, bro!

Noloyiso Mtembu: I remember witnessing a lingering kiss between you two in her old car outside City Campus ???? after that you were dreamy the whole Political Science lecture. It was beautiful to watch. The kiss, I mean.

Thulisile Ngunelihle Qwabe: What a love story, I just can't wait for the fifth wedding, this is so touchy, and you and your family are blessed to have such a wife.

7

Honeymoon for three!

I owe my English wife a honeymoon. Yes, despite an avalanche of marriage ceremonies, we have never had an official honeymoon. You read that right: a Zulu boy candidly admits that he has never given his English wife a proper honeymoon. Let this fact sink in. I am not ashamed of this oversight. My English wife is a staunch believer in the proverb that says all good things come to those who wait. Nevertheless, it appears to me that there has never been anything conventional about my interracial marriage.

As you have read, this interracial marriage thingy is fraught with peril. While I was fully aware of this from the outset, nothing could prepare me for a marriage ceremony ending without, yes, a happy ending. I know what you're thinking: this seventeen-year-old romantic endeavour is nothing but fast-paced farce. Facts don't support this fallacy. I love my wife and my life with her. It's an adrenaline rush of a slightly different kind.

Yet I do believe that this interracial union was blighted from the start. At first, it was my clumsy marriage proposal made late in the night in a state of beer-induced bravado. Yes, I proposed marriage to my girlfriend after 11 p.m. one mundane Friday night. Lights were out. She was probably dozing off.

I blurted out: 'Perhaps we should just get married when we are in Mauritius.'

She woke from her slumber and faced me in the dark. 'Are you proposing?' she asked.

I was at a loss for words. I mumbled something about having a romantic wedding on the beach in a foreign land. We had already booked and paid for a summer holiday at Preskil Beach Resort in Mauritius. Don't ask me: since when do Zulu boys elope for their big days? Anyway, I am made of sterner stuff.

I made up for my clumsy marriage proposal within a week. In a highly sophisticated secret mission, I drove to our favourite restaurant, Moyo uShaka in Durban, to arrange for a special dinner for two. Moyo uShaka is a uniquely Durban destination offering the perfect place in which to relax and watch the world go by. At Moyo uShaka, you can enjoy cocktails at the beach bar, exquisite views of the Indian Ocean, tropical weather, exotic flavours and soulful vibes. This particular Moyo restaurant offers Africa at its laid-back best, so the brochure says – and it's true. It was just the tonic that my clumsiness required. My brief to the Moyo manager was simple: go the extra mile. I explained that it was a high-level, secret mission. I demanded all the bells and whistles associated with a marriage-proposal dinner. I booked the babysitter and made sure that the woman of the hour was free at the appointed date and time.

With their meticulous planning, Moyo went to town. Starters: check. Mains: check. Bottle of champagne: check. Flowers: check. Makeshift temporary ring: check. Zulu dancers: check. Desserts: check. Smile and be merry: check. In short, I went the whole hog, like a true professional. You see, it helps to watch television and have an active imagination. The whole evening was punctuated by song and dance. And, yes, in the midst of a Zulu dance, I went down on one knee and I popped the question. She said yes, yes, and yes. But I digress.

Here is the genesis of my beer-induced marriage proposal. Some time earlier, at 5 p.m., a colleague and friend and I were sitting at the bar having cold beers. We looked at our phones simultaneously at exactly 5 p.m. We knew the drill by then. At exactly 5 p.m., our then girlfriends – known by an innocuous nickname, the Where Are You? Club – would call and, yes, their first words would be: 'Where are you?' We had two prepared answers: Just waiting in line to see our political principal to approve our speech, or just waiting for the procurement guys to finalise our purchase order for tomorrow's event. I am unable to confirm or deny that this was always a lie. So, after receiving our customary 5 p.m. phone calls, we had an intense and robust discussion about the future of our Where Are You? Club members.

After careful consideration of all facts presented before us, we resolved as follows: That the Where Are You? Club is a nice bunch of beautiful and thoughtful girls who deserved better in life. We resolved, therefore, to change their status from single to married. The following orders were made: a) the singleness of the Where Are You? Club members is reviewed and set aside; b) they are granted direct access to our hearts; and c) they shall be spared the costs associated with the changing of their single status. It was decreed that they should be married without undue delay after following the strict observance of the rules and all rituals associated with marriage proposals. We have so ruled.

My dearest colleague, who shall remain nameless, complied with our order within three months. Yes, in fewer than three months, he pulled it off. Boom! He was married.

My big day came in January the following year after fervent preparations, including finding a wedding planner in the foreign

land. We had to quickly acquaint ourselves with the legal require-
ments of getting married in Mauritius. After months of preparations,
January 2008 came, and it was a case of all roads lead to Rome. We
arrived in Mauritius ready to tie the knot. We had already had our
antenuptial contract signed and lodged with the authorities in South
Africa. In terms of Mauritian law, we had to state our intention to
marry before Mauritian Home Affairs so that it could be displayed
in public to allow for any objections. Strangely, there were none.

The second leg involved a trek to Port Louis, the capital city of
Mauritius, where the High Court is located. We had to appear before
a High Court judge to make our official vows: that there were no
impediments to our nuptials and, of course, that we were of sane
mind and understood fully the consequences of our marriage.

When all the preliminaries had been sorted out, it was time for
Linda, the hotel's wedding planner, to take over. She booked sessions
for my wife's grooming regime and fixed the time of the wedding at
3 p.m. The date was to be 15 January 2008. She had convinced us
earlier to spend R1 000 on a floral decoration for the archway. She
hired a professional French photographer. At exactly 3 p.m., it was
all set to go. But there was a snag: for a few minutes, the bride was
nowhere to be seen. She had apparently got stuck in a grooming
session, and was late for her own wedding.

We had agreed that, as per Mauritian law, our wedding would
be a public affair – except we had no guests. Yes, it's still possible to
get married without inviting the whole neighbourhood, Facebook
friends, Twitter followers, varsity friends, work colleagues, in-laws,
aunties, family and extended family. We neither created a Facebook
event nor checked in at the beach. It was a serene affair. Linda had
set up a podium on the beach at the edge of the Indian Ocean, with
our colourful floral arrangement displayed on the archway.

Our Mauritian Home Affairs official, clearly a man of high moral rectitude, was on time and on point. He conducted the ceremony with the aplomb of a true professional. As you now know, we had concocted our own vows. We signed on the dotted line. It was all over in fifteen minutes. Our only guest was Miss N. We then engaged in that most important ritual of newlyweds, the photo shoot. It was more interesting and lively than our fifteen minutes of fame. The abiding memory the photos captured for posterity is the exquisite background of the Indian Ocean.

After the photo-shoot ritual, we prepared ourselves for a night never to forget. Of course, the hotel had planned a full dinner for two with a specially selected menu, wine of choice, and a lot of giggling by the newlyweds. After easy conversation and copious consumption of alcoholic beverages, we retired to our bedroom after 10 p.m. Then, it hit home: our daughter would be sleeping in the same bedroom. When we arrived, she nonchalantly demanded her routine: reading before bedtime, and her other rituals. In case you missed it, our daughter was sharing a bedroom with us. It did put a damper on things. Hence, honeymoon for three.

So, truth be told, I am yet to go on a real honeymoon with my wife. I owe her one. Ten years is a long time in the merry dance. My only consolation is deep inside my bag of Zulu idioms – *isinamuva liyabukwa*, loosely translated to mean 'he who dances last gets all the attention'. As if having a honeymoon for three wasn't enough of a setback, in the morning we discovered that someone had stolen our archway flowers. Before the wedding, someone had stolen our beach towels, which belonged to the hotel. We had to pay R1 000 to replace the towels, yet the hotel washed its hands of the matter of our archway flowers' disappearing act.

8

Introducing my English wife to my Zulu ancestors

I am not getting married to my English wife again anytime soon. Yes, folks, the whirlwind wedding-ceremonies wagon came to a screeching halt on the 2016 Easter weekend. You will recall that I still owed my parents and my village a traditional and a white wedding.

No, stupid. I didn't have the two outstanding wedding ceremonies over the Easter weekend, but something of Shakespearean proportions (except it wasn't a tragedy) happened while I was visiting my family down in Zululand. Let's just say for now that my family is no longer looking forward to the two outstanding wedding ceremonies. Don't get ahead of yourself and pronounce that sanity has prevailed: I have learnt to be extra cautious when dealing with my parents.

This is how the story goes. We spent the 2016 Easter weekend with my parents in Ulundi in the northern part of KwaZulu-Natal. Ulundi, in the heart of Zululand, is set among marvellous hills and the rough valleys of the White Umfolozi River. The former capital of the Zulu Kingdom, it straddles Route 66 between Nongoma and Melmoth. We arrived on Friday afternoon. Our trip to Ulundi was an ordinary courtesy visit to see my family. In tow, I had my English wife, mixed-race daughter and son born of a Xhosa-speaking mother. My village is now used to seeing a white woman among them, so it's no longer an event worth gossiping about.

However, as a well-nurtured Zulu boy, I had sent some money to my mother so that she could buy the ingredients required for brewing the traditional Zulu beer known as *umqombothi*. This was a small gesture on my part to the ancestors in acknowledgement of their presence in my life: what better way to do so than to give them something to drink and be merry about. There was no customary slaughter of a beast or goat.

This visit was meant to be as routine as possible. It turned out to be anything but.

Firstly, on the Saturday, my wife entered the Mncubes' kitchen for the very first time with the sole intention of playing *makoti*, which meant cooking for the in-laws. This had taken her some sixteen long years to do. I had decided in the week leading up to our visit that it was the time and place for my wife to break with tradition once and for all. You see, in my family tradition, unless the bride has officially been introduced to the ancestors through the slaughter of a beast, she can't perform *makoti* duties, including cooking.

Despite my spirit of defiance, there was another snag. There were sixteen mouths to feed. Nonetheless, my wife took to the cooking task like a duck to water. After an epic six-hour cooking session with a malfunctioning electric stove, food was delivered to all. I patted her on the back for a job well done. My parents remained mum on the breaking of tradition. For the past sixteen years, my wife has been treated as a visitor to be served meals at appointed times.

On Sunday, the cooking session had to be repeated. Of course, this was now routine for my wife.

But something monumental was in the offing. While I was seated outside one of the huts and whiling away the time sharing banter with my mom, other family members and hangers-on, my father joined us. He looked apprehensive. I witnessed the perspiration running down his neck. At once, he demanded that all of my family join us. I offered a reprieve for my wife and daughter, saying they were busy cooking. My mother also chipped in to say it wasn't necessary. My father would have none of it. He shouted my mother down. Everybody had to come, because he wanted to do something very important. Sensing I wasn't going to win the battle, let alone the war, I ordered some random kid to go and summon my wife and daughter. They descended upon the place at once. I didn't make any eye contact with my wife, fearing that she would ask me what was going on and I was none the wiser.

My father, in his petulant fashion, made no small talk, but got straight down to business. He announced matter-of-factly that he was already late in his appointed task of speaking to *amadlozi* about my side of the family. In Zulu, *amadlozi* means ancestors (*idlozi* is the singular form). It means a human spirit, or the soul of the departed. As he is wont to do, he walked metres away from us to be near *isibaya* (the kraal) and started *ukuthetha idlozi* like a house on fire. *Ukuthetha idlozi* means 'to scold'. Zulu historians argue that *ukuthetha idlozi* linguistically gives one the initial impression of an aggressive kind of relationship between the ancestors and their descendants. In practice, it is not so – the literal translation is misleading. *Ukuthetha idlozi* is an expression that implies praying to the ancestors, in a way that is not to be confused with religious prayer. It is like a senior counsel's prayer before a judge. In its traditional meaning, *ukuthetha idlozi* refers to the communication between the ancestors and their descendants. Basically, you tell them what they ought to know, and possibly make special requests. We treat the dead like the living, except that we attach greater value to our relationship with them. We are Zulus – that's just how we roll.

After a beautiful rendition of *izithakazelo*, meaning praises attached to a particular group (in this case, the Mncubes) in which the clan's forebears are also referred to, my father proudly reported thus:

I am reporting to you MaZilakatha [the Mncubes' praise name] that uBhekisisa, the son of MaMlambo [my mother's maiden name], is now married. He has two children. I appeal to you to guard and protect his new family. We pray for their good health, wealth and peace. My apologies for only telling you this now. It happened a while back.

My father ought to have performed this ritual of *ukuthetha idlozi* in 2008, when I got married. Nonetheless, the eagerness with which he took to the task, albeit nine years later, made me chuckle. He even dispensed with the tradition of burning *impepho*, a plant offering to the spirits of the departed. It opens communication with the ancestors and makes any request, report or sacrifice acceptable. It is normally a precursor to *ukuthetha idlozi*. I couldn't have cared less: I was just happy to hear my father say the words, 'uBhekisisa is now married.'

So, dear reader, it has come to pass that my proverbial English wife, Professor D., is now officially united with my Zulu ancestors. By all accounts, the message to the ancestors was accepted. In simple terms, it means my wife has been accepted as a *makoti* by the Mncube clan after the official reportage to *amadlozi*. This despite the fact that there was no sacrificial slaughter of a beast and subsequent traditional wedding. As my father has relented and introduced my wife to the *amadlozi*, it means she is officially regarded as a daughter of the Mncube clan. She can now milk the cows, cook the food and basically be sent on errands by my family as a duly wedded wife.

Sadly, in reality, this means that there are zero prospects for any further wedding ceremonies.

READERS' RESPONSES

Pippa Davies: Natural storyteller!! Newspaper fodder??

Mmanaledi Mataboge-Mashetla: Talk about cheating the ancestors and being helped to get away with it. I'm waiting for that book so I can review it properly. Sounds interesting already.

Dumisani Zondi: It is such an engrossing read indeed. People like Fred Khumalo know a good bookable story when they see one. Don't waste anyone's time and do like you have been ordered and release a book! We want it before you get your land back.

Thuli Nhlapo: Beautiful read. Thoroughly enjoyed reading it.

Sphiwe Maphumulo: Good piece. Please produce a book out of these experiences. I will be the first one to buy.

Marie-Sylvie Rushton: Can't wait for the book.

Sthembile Ma-Ngubane Tshikosi: I can't wait to read the book?? This was definitely a good appetiser.

9

Quagmire: Negotiating cultural expression in the interracial marriage

I am a firm believer in my Zulu culture. My very being is embodied in the cultural expression, belief system and habits of the Zulu people. I am an adherent of the belief in *amadlozi* as a basis of my spiritual being. I believe in uMveliqangi (the one who came first), the African God of Creation, as opposed to the Christian Holy Trinity. When I lurched across the colour line to marry an Englishwoman, I didn't forgo my Zulu cultural roots – well, at least in theory.

As you know by now, my wife is English. For the race-obsessed South African public, she is a white South African woman. She is a Catholic, although she was excommunicated in the 1980s for her anti-apartheid activism. But to this day, she yearns for the Catholic Mass. I guess you can't put a good Catholic down. As far as I have ascertained in the past seventeen years of our courtship, she and her family don't believe in ancestors. It appears they have no cultural expression, belief system or habits, barring those that are rooted in Christianity. I may be wrong, but what I do know for sure is that my wife's belief system and habits are diametrically opposed to all key features of the Zulu culture.

For instance, my Zulu culture is deeply rooted in the slaughter of domestic livestock for food and as part of ancestral ceremonies:

to appease the ancestors, as it were. My wife, a vegetarian and a fervent anti-animal-slaughter activist, is opposed to animal slaughter for any reason, including for food consumption or as a sacrifice to the ancestors. This explains why we haven't yet performed the *imbeleko* ceremony for my daughter.

In this minefield of cultural dissonance, my daughter is left alone to navigate her cultural incongruity. For starters, many people want to refer to her as a coloured. What the race-obsessed paratroopers forget is that coloured identity is a social construct foisted upon people by the apartheid regime. Generally, during apartheid's madness, people had to be classified as so-called coloured. With the passage of time, some people embraced their coloured identity. So, nobody is born into the coloured identity. It is a matter of choice. My point of departure is that there is an urgent need for a paradigm shift in terms of cultural identity. We must, without further hesitation, re-imagine the whole discourse of apartheid-inspired cultural identity politics.

My daughter has already freed herself of the coloured tag. In terms of cultural identity, she is veering towards the Zulu culture – at least in terms of attire and language. She is judiciously learning the Zulu language and is the top student in her class. All she really craves is to have a conversation in Zulu with her *gogo* (grandmother) and her many cousins. At some stage during her short school career, she rejected learning Afrikaans, claiming in her young mind that 'It is irrelevant and spoken only by a few Afrikaners.' Having declared herself a suburban Zulu girl, she asked me to buy her Zulu attire for Heritage Day celebrations. My mother beat me to it when we visited home, presenting my daughter with full Zulu attire made of beadwork. My daughter has made it very clear that she wants to sound like and dress the part of a Zulu girl. I am yet to introduce her to the actual intricacies of being Zulu. In terms of animal slaughter, she strongly believes in humane animal treatment, yet she loves her chicken. She has tasted red meat and is not too keen on it. We have not prescribed what she may or may not eat. So, she is half-vegetarian and half-carnivore.

As a testimony to the new cosmopolitan future we have envisioned for our daughter, we have given her three different names. Her first name represents her Zuluness and freedom, her second reflects her French/Mauritian side, and her third is her mother's surname. We consider her as having agency. It is high time society gives her the space and time neccssary to negotiate her cultural path and identity, unimpeded by the ghosts of apartheid past.

In terms of my culture, my wife and I ought to have performed a series of prenuptial ceremonies culminating in the traditional wedding. Yet, we didn't necessarily jump through the hoops to seal our matrimonial arrangement. On our marriage, my wife was meant to take my surname. She didn't. So, there is no Mrs Mncube in our household. This is just one of the many cultural anomalies in our interracial matrimony. The most significant cultural mismatch, however, comes with what ought to have happened *before* we made our vows.

Firstly, I skipped the sacred tradition of paying *lobola. Lobola* is generally described as a bride price, traditionally one the groom pays in cattle to the bride's family. Generally, it is the equivalent of eleven cattle for a virgin girl – loosely meaning, a girl without a child. However, *lobola* can vary from family to family or clan to clan. Hence, the whole process is termed *lobola* negotiations. *Lobola* doesn't necessarily have to be paid in cattle. During the negotiations, the elders can agree on a monetary price. Assuming that my wife's family could have opted for monetary compensation, in today's terms I would have paid a minimum of R7 000 in lieu of each cow to my English wife's family. But, in terms of her culture, there was no expectation that I would pay anything. So, I got away with cultural murder.

Secondly, I didn't offer my in-laws *izibizo*. These are gifts expressly requested by the bride's family to be paid for by the groom. *Izibizo* and *lobola* negotiations happen simultaneously. However, a day is set aside for *izibizo* in a mini ceremony symbolising the strengthening of relations between the two families. There's always the slaughter of an animal, and feasting accompanied by *umqombothi*.

The third leg in this process is the one that is a sore point for my family, especially my mom. It is called *umbondo*, and is normally the last event before a traditional wedding takes place. This is where the bride reciprocates by buying a variety of gifts for the groom's family. These range from groceries and appliances to blankets, and so on. My wife didn't do this for her in-laws. To this day, it is a festering wound for my mother. *Umbondo* is usually a big and colourful ceremony during which, as per the dictates of Zulu culture, a beast is slaughtered and *umqombothi* is brewed for the occasion.

My wife, for her sins, also missed out on the ceremony known as *umembeso*. In her master's thesis titled 'Assessing Politeness, Language and Gender in Hlonipha', Thobekile Patience Luthuli explains, in detail, the significance and process of *umembeso*. She writes that, when you *mbesa* something or someone, you cover that thing or person with something. In Zulu culture, *umembeso* is when the groom's family takes gifts to the bride's family to say thank you for the gift of their new daughter in-law. It is important to note that the purpose of *umembeso* is for the in-laws to show their future daughter-in-law how they want her to dress. So, the most important part of the ceremony is a brand-new wardrobe for the bride.

The ceremony can be seen as the equivalent of *izibizo*, except that the roles are reversed. It is the turn of the bride's family to receive gifts. A list of gifts and their respective recipients is provided to the groom's family ahead of time. The type of gifts requested will generally include blankets, pinafores, head scarves, clothes, food, straw mats, and sometimes a live goat. More than just the handing over of gifts, *umembeso* is a celebration, with dancing and the slaughtering of animals. The arrival of the groom's family is greeted with song and dance at the gate to the bride's family home. Both families compete in song, with the groom's family asking for permission to enter the yard by announcing that they have come bearing gifts. Traditionally, a goat is prepared by the bride's family as a way of welcoming the groom's family to their home and, in some instances, small gifts will also be given to the groom's family.

A moot point for my family and my mom is the final leg of this process, known as *umabo*. *Umabo* can best be described as a Zulu traditional wedding, which usually takes place after the white wedding, if the parties elected to have one. It is believed that one is not fully married in accordance with Zulu culture unless one has gone through the process of *umabo*. *Umabo* is similar to *umembeso* in the sense that bespoke gifts are ordered by the groom's family to be delivered on the day of the traditional wedding. It is a chance for the bride to shower her in-laws with gifts to their heart's desire. But the process is too involved.

During the *umabo* ceremony, the bride's family should slaughter a goat for her and burn *impepho* to tell the ancestors that their daughter is going to become a member of another family. After the wedding, the groom's family should welcome her with a goat. For *umabo*, the two families slaughter cows (one from each family) and exchange certain parts of the meat.

Umabo always takes place at the groom's family residence; the bride brings with her some gifts as per the list and wishes of the groom's family. On the day of the ceremony, the bride must wear traditional clothes – *isidwaba* (a skirt made from cow skin for married women) and *isicholo* (to cover the head) – and she needs to cover her shoulders. The bride is to sit on a grass mat and, as a sign of *hlonipha* (respect), should not look at or talk to anyone. The bride must bring with her a kist, and a bed with pillows and linen; she must bring grass mats, pillows and blankets for her in-laws (the groom's family sends a list so that, when the day of *umabo* arrives, the bride knows whom to give blankets to). Everybody on the list is given a variety of gifts, from grass mats to pillows and blankets.

Umabo is a very important ritual. It brings families together and, in the process, the bride is told what is expected of her from her family and her in-laws. It is believed that this tradition is the way in which the ancestors recognise the bride. It is also a beautiful tradition where people can showcase their traditional attire, and sing and dance. It brings all the different elements of Zulu culture together in one big ceremony.

The traditional wedding is a colourful affair, complete with traditional music, Zulu dance and, of course, feasting, coupled with *umqombothi* flowing. On the last day of the wedding, the *ukuyala* occurs, which means 'to advise'. This is a meeting of the bridal party, the groom's party and several elders from both families. With the families present, the bride and groom are counselled on the importance of keeping the new family together according to the dictates of Zulu culture, custom and habits.

According to my mother, despite having had four wedding ceremonies, we fail the Zulu cultural test qualifying us as a properly married couple. But my father has relented after nine long years, and introduced my wife to the ancestors without all these pre- and postnuptial ceremonies.

10

The stuff of dreams: Dreaming in the interracial marriage

Having been born with a caul, I have psychic abilities that manifest mainly through dreams.

In isiZulu, to dream is *ukuphupha* (adjective) or *iphupho* (noun). *Ukuphupha* is akin to experiencing real-life drama in a film-like setting while you're in a deep sleep. The event in a dream is unknown to the minds of mere mortals. It manifests in your dream via culturally specific symbolism. The key to this *ukuphupha* process is that you must be in a position to remember the finer details of the entire dream, as it unfolded. In Zulu clture, *ukuphupha* with a purpose is reserved for people with an awakened spiritual connection to the other side, the world of the ancestors.

In Zulu dreamology, everything is deeply rooted in Zulu culture, custom and habits. Thus, the interpretation of Zulu dreams is not universal. Zulu dreamology is diametrically opposed to Sigmund Freud's work in dream analyses. Freud argued that the repository of knowledge lies in our unconscious mind and that, through psychoanalysis, one can make the unconscious conscious. Generally, psychologists suggest that our dreams may be the mind's way of alerting us to unresolved issues. Yet, for us as Africans – especially Zulus – dreams are a direct communication between the dead and the living. African traditional healers, such as the traditional healing expert Sangoma Gogo Moyo, confirm that dreams are a platform for communication with our ancestors.

My mother is a faith healer with psychic abilities, a gift bestowed upon her at birth by her ancestors. As a result, she is skilled in Zulu dream interpretation and can understand premonitions according to the Zulu culture, custom and belief system. The skill of dream analysis is passed down from generation to generation through oral history. There are few people who have the gift of dreaming dreams that have any meaning in real life; you must have psychic abilities bestowed upon you at birth. I learnt the skill of dream interpretation through narrating, in detail, my dreams to my mother. The key to understanding meaningful dreams is to become imbued with knowledge of their symbolism. For instance, if you dream about getting married, it means the opposite: death.

Dear reader, please be patient and work with me here. First, I must unpack the key meanings of Zulu dreams and their significance before I navigate the difficulties of dreaming within an interracial marriage.

I first realised that I had the gift of meaningful dreams and psychic abilities in 1989. I dreamt that it was raining at school. It seemed like an innocuous dream, until I told my mother about it the next morning. She explained that rain signifies tears. To my surprise, she boldly said that something bad would happen to the principal. That very morning at school assembly, we were informed that the principal had been in a car accident and that his wife had died in its aftermath. I was shocked. I had not realised the magnitude of my psychic powers until that fateful morning. As the news sank in, I knew I was different. To this day, I remember that dream as if it happened yesterday.

Over the years, I have had many dreams that have, sadly, come true. I vividly remember the year South Africa lost its bid to host the 2000 Olympics; I knew the night before that we had not made it. I told a fellow with whom I shared a flat, one Mr Langa Nzuza. When the news broke at midday, he was the first to call me to share his shock that my dream had come true.

As another example, in 1998 I dreamt about my first graduation at the then Technikon Natal. In the dream, I arrived late and saw the former Minister of Education, Professor Sibusiso Bhengu. In 2004, when I finally graduated, the same scenes replayed themselves in real life, except for the presence of Professor Bhengu – I was late for my graduation, as per the 1998 dream. According to the standard interpretation of Zulu dreams, a graduation gown also signifies a great luck or a breakthrough.

I regularly dream of kings, queens and presidents. My mom told me in the 1980s that this is a sign of good luck. Without fail, if I dream of the revered Nelson Mandela, I know for certain that luck is on my side. In November 2014, I dreamt about chatting to President Mandela. The very next morning, the Minister of Basic Education, Mrs Angie Motshekga, decided to extend my one-year employment contract to five years. I was thrilled.

Generally, dreaming of kings, queens and presidents means that whichever venture is uppermost in your mind is set to run smoothly. And yes, before you ask, I do dream about President Jacob Zuma. In dreamland, he still commands the respect accorded to all presidents, despite being vilified in real life. Two weeks before I landed the publishing contract for this book, I saw President Zuma in a dream, visiting my household. I knew something big was in the offing, and boom! – within ten days, I had landed a book-publishing deal. Clearly, this project is endorsed by my ancestors.

Another significant symbol in Zulu dreamology is nakedness. If in a dream I see myself naked in a public place, it means I am likely to be exposed to danger in real life. I have had several of these warnings over the years. And yes, after having such a dream, things do go cock-eyed for a while, until the cycle turns. Strangely, if my wife dreams something similar, it's meaningless.

Here is a more recent and extraordinary example: On the eve of joining the KwaZulu-Natal Department of Education in October 2013, I had a dream in which I saw many snakes. It was scary. I woke up in panic mode, sweating. The most significant part of the dream was that I didn't manage to kill any of the snakes. My mother had drilled it into me that seeing a snake or snakes in a dream can mean only one thing: your enemies are gaining the upper hand. She told me that it is always better to kill a snake in a dream than to be scared and run away. To say my tenure at the KwaZulu-Natal Department of Education was laborious is to put it mildly. Many a staff member gossiped about me and engaged in backbiting. At one point, all the staff members in the MEC's office, barring two, ganged up on me and threatened the security of my tenure. In short, most people hated me for absolutely nothing that can be explained by mere mortals.

I had been warned, yet I remained shockingly unprepared for the onslaught. Truth is, to this day I don't know where such venom came from. It got so bad that, at one stage, 90 per cent of the people in the MEC's office weren't on speaking terms with me. The hatred continued beyond my tenure, when one senior manager wrote to my new political principal at the Basic Education ministry, badmouthing me. Talk about dreams coming true. If all things were equal, I could have taken up the matter with my ancestors and slaughtered a goat or two to ask them to repel my enemies. I didn't; today, I am the wiser for it.

The other striking feature of my dreams is death, death and more death. I have lost count of the people (family members, acquaintances and friends) I dreamt about who were alive at the time, but whose days I knew were numbered. In less than a year of having had the dream, they died. In my dream, I will see the person dressed in new clothes, having built a new house, or getting married. A long time ago, my mother explained to me that dreaming this means that death is imminent. After my half-brother got married and his wife fell pregnant, I remember having a vivid dream in which his wife was wearing new clothes. Her newborn died within a year.

Since I've been married to my English wife, I have not stopped dreaming meaningful dreams. I tell her about them. She finds the whole Zulu dream-interpretation thingy bewildering. At first, she didn't believe in dreams that have meaning in real life. However, with the passage of time, she has, at least, become a trusted partner in lending me her ear regarding my dreams. She is beginning to gain better insight into the working world of Zulu ancestors and dreams. She also dreams at night, as most people do. But we both laugh off her dreams.

However, there has been some consternation in the dream world since my interracial marriage. Frankly, the interpretation of some dreams is beginning to make no sense at all. First on the list is that, according to my mother, dreaming about a white person is a sign of evil spirits. Evil spirits are associated with immediate danger, and could mean that one of your ancestors has gone rogue. Yes, through the process of witchcraft, an ancestor can be turned against his or her own. Anyway, I digress.

Picture this. Here I am with my white wife in a dream. Does it mean that, in my dreams, my wife represents an evil spirit? My mom is none the wiser. Yes, now and then, when I see random white people in my dreams, a thing or two goes awry in real life. But towards the end of the writing of this book, the unthinkable happened: I saw my English wife in a dream for the first time in sixteen years. And nothing went wrong afterwards.

But the real trouble with meaningful dreams in an interracial marriage is that I am not allowed a follow-through. Let me give you an example. If I dream of snakes, as I have explained, in real life I can perform a ritual known as *ukwesheleza emadlozini* to ask my ancestors to repel the imminent danger. As they say, forewarned is forearmed. This means there must be a ceremony complete with *ukuthetha idlozi*, the burning of *impepho*, the brewing of *umqombothi* (for which my wife has no recipe to this day) and the slaughter of a goat. In addition, to perform such a ritual successfully, I need access to *umsamo* – that sacred place where communication between the living and the ancestors takes place. In our suburban home, there is no *umsamo*. Any thought of slaughtering a goat is a non-starter, considering our location – Waterkloof Ridge, Pretoria – the SPCA and my wife's aversion to killing animals. I am stuck between a rock and a hard place.

Complicating matters further is that now, I actually do have a white ancestor watching over me. In 2013, during a routine consultation with my faith healer, Sis Dora, she revealed to me that an elderly white male was opening his hands to give me good luck. I spoke to my wife about this premonition and, through the process of elimination, we zeroed in on her grandfather from her mother's side. We traced his grave to a cemetery in the suburb of Morningside in Durban. Unfortunately, the cemetery is old, and permanently under lock and key. I ought to have gone to the old man's grave to pay my respects and perhaps leave a gift, such as flowers, or found a way inside and cleaned up the grave. Since I couldn't perform any ritual for the old man, I am not sure if he is still holding his hands open to give me a fortune. That said, however, how on earth can I be sure that the next time I dream of a white male he is not a sign of an evil spirit, but my elderly white ancestor about to bestow some luck on me?

Another perplexing issue is that all meaningful dreams are in my mother tongue, despite the fact that English has been my language of choice since 1993. I have only dreamt once in English. The other snag is the location. At least 99 per cent of my dreams are located in the Eshowe district, where my umbilical cord lies buried deep beneath the soil. My family relocated from Eshowe to Ulundi in 1997, yet the location of my dreams has remained constant. The only time I saw the family's Ulundi household in a dream was when we were moving back to Eshowe.

Finally, as I've written, I just want to be reclassified as a white man. Perhaps I will then be freed from the clutches of my ancestors. I don't know – maybe one day I will stop dreaming meaningful dreams. I wouldn't mind being permanently excused from perform-ing Zulu cultural rituals. I yearn to be a complete Zulu cultural delinquent – with the permission of my Zulu ancestors, of course. *Thokoza Dlozi!*

11

Animal slaughter held in abeyance to introduce my daughter to the ancestors

My daughter, Miss N., has not been officially introduced to my Zulu ancestors. As far as Zulu custom is concerned, she is persona non grata. You see, my daughter is a product of my current marriage to an English wife. In her mother's culture, there is no ritual to be performed for the newborn, whereas in my culture, there must be *ukuchithwa kwegazi* (spilling of the blood or slaughtering of an animal) to welcome her into the world of the living and introduce her to the world of the ancestors.

The name of the ritual is called *imbeleko*. The *imbeleko* ceremony is a celebration to introduce and welcome a newborn child, although occasionally even an adult newcomer may be introduced to both the living and the ancestral spirits. According to historians, Zulus regard the *imbeleko* ceremony as a necessity for every child in the family.

In reality, I must slaughter a goat to officially introduce my daughter to her ancestors. This ritual, in its historical sense, is a family celebration and a gesture of hospitality, conveying the message that the new member of the family is welcomed by both the living members of the family as well as the ancestors. This is a once-off ritual in the Zulu culture, unlike the birthday party in Western culture. It should also not be confused with the Western classical

Christian tradition of a christening. Zulus firmly believe that the newborn is a special gift from the ancestors, just like Christians hold on to the belief that a child is a blessing from God.

I have not performed this ritual of *imbeleko* for my daughter – or any ritual, for that matter. My daughter has never experienced the slaughter of any animal. To make matters worse, if I were to perform the ritual for my daughter, she would have to *ukuphulula imbuzi*, meaning to stroke or rub the goat very gently while the elder of the family is communicating with the ancestors. My daughter is sort of an animal activist: I can't imagine her stroking a goat that will eventually be brutally killed in her honour. As with her mother, I don't think killing an animal in her name will go down very well. She is a sensitive soul like that. I have not even broached the subject with her.

My quandary is that my culture calls for indiscriminate animal sacrifice. I know this for real, as it was demanded of me by my ancestors later in my life. The ritual was performed for me when I was in my late twenties, after I had contracted an ill-defined illness.

This is how the story goes. In 1994, I fell critically ill with an unknown ailment. I went to a medical doctor who, after some probing and examination, gave me a clean bill of health, despite persistent stabbing and throbbing pains in my body. The pains persisted for some time, until I did as most of my people would do: I went to see a sangoma. She told me that my parents hadn't performed *imbeleko* for me. Complicating matters further is that I was born with a caul. So, not only did my parents forgo the custom of *imbeleko*, but they didn't perform the thanksgiving for *ukuzalwa ngembethe* either. They were supposed to have performed the traditional *imbeleko* ceremony while specifically expressing their gratitude that I was a special kid.

In short, my ancestors were angry that they had given my parents a special gift which they had never acknowledged. I went home and reported this to my mother. She immediately told me that it was true. She went to report this to my father, and, on the same day, the *imbeleko* preparations began in earnest.

First, my mother had to brew *umqombothi*. Three days later, the proper ritual began. This involved burning *impepho*. *Impepho* is burnt during the process of *uthetha idlozi*, when there is a rendition of clan names (*izithakazelo*). There is live communication between the living and the ancestors while *impepho* burns. It is believed that *impepho* helps to connect the ancestors with the living, assisting the living in talking to the ancestors about the upcoming ritual (*ukuthetha idlozi*) and to apologise for it not having happened earlier (*ukushweleza edlozini*). After *ukuthetha idlozi* and *ukushweleza*, a goat is slaughtered as an offering to the ancestors. The rest is history; the whole village comes for *umqombothi* and the family feasts on goat's meat. After this ritual was performed, I miraculously recovered.

During the *imbeleko* ceremony, an altar, known as *umsamo*, is created and decorated with food, treats and *umqombothi*. Generally, *umsamo* is located away from the doorway inside a hut. It is where things like beer pots are placed, and where the goat is hung after it has been slaughtered and skinned. It is generally believed that the visiting ancestral spirits also reside at the *umsamo*. Essentially, the *umsamo* is a designated place for interceding with the ancestors. Every Zulu household is required to have this special hut with *umsamo* as its special feature. It is regarded as a sacred place to which only the elders (mostly males) and nominated persons have access. No one is allowed to wear shoes near *umsamo*. You are required to be barefoot and and on your knees.

After the *imbeleko* ceremony, the child must wear *isiphandla*. *Isiphandla* is a goat-skin bangle worn as a symbol that the correct ritual has been performed. Historians describe *isiphandla* as an armlet of a hide worn by the particular person for whom the goat was slaughtered. Africans wear *isiphandla* for many traditional purposes – especially Zulus, who practise their tradition of and belief in ancestors. It is made from the skin taken from the goat's leg. In Zulu culture, a female wears *isiphandla* on the left wrist, and the male wears it on the right. One may not cut it off without informing the ancestors; it has to fall off naturally. The *inyongo* or bile that is taken from the goat is squirted on the *isiphandla* to create a connection with the ancestors. *Isiphandla* can be seen as the physical link between you and your ancestors.

After *imbeleko*, the slaughtered goat is taken to the *umsamo*, where it stays overnight. The next morning, the animal is cooked and shared at a feast with family and friends. The *isiphandla* will have a meaty smell to it for weeks, which can be covered up by dusting it with flour.

When I was growing up, I wore many an *isiphandla*. I was never ashamed of my *isiphandla*, although I had no knowledge about its higher purpose.

I guess at some point I will have to perform two rituals: *ukushweleza edlozini* to apologise to the ancestors for not having performed the *imbeleko* ritual for my daughter earlier, and the actual *imbeleko* ceremony itself to introduce my offspring – finally – to her rightful ancestors.

12

Death and grieving in the interracial marriage

I often joke that I want to die as a Muslim or a Jew. This is particularly because of the swift burial rites in both Islam and Judaism. However, I am a Zulu boy. If I die while my parents are still alive, there will be fireworks – death-ritual warfare between them and my English wife. The whole death thingy will wreak havoc within these families (I think). All will be left floundering as they seek to navigate this cultural maelstrom. As researchers on funeral rites have correctly reminded us, the process of mourning is a culturally patterned, visible expression of the bereaved's thoughts and feelings.

For my family, there is a Zulu cultural manual that determines such things as the slaughtering of the beast, the mourning dress, mourning period and the cleansing ceremonies. However, my part of the family with the English wife is culturally neutral. In fact, we are not staunch followers of any discernible cultural belief system. As for me, I live in two worlds – the one of my extended family, complete with a Zulu cultural manual for all major life events, and my culturally neutral, nuclear family. I have mentioned before that I feel like a Zulu cultural delinquent.

The first question will be the location of my grave. Should I be buried in my ancestral home next to my ancestors, or next to my wife and, eventually, children, in the urban cemetery? The second most pressing question will be which mourning ritual to adopt. My English wife will certainly want a low-cost and quick burial rite, according to some Catholic traditions. My family would prefer a more elaborate Zulu traditional rite.

Within the Zulu cultural context, the dead are regarded as ancestors and treated with great respect, as they are believed to have a special relationship with the living. It should be noted that, in African culture in general, and in Zulu culture in particular, death is not an event that just occurs, is handled and then forgotten about. When one dies, a series of events usually takes place. These may include a pre-burial mourning period, delivering the funeral rites accompanied by feasting, and post-burial ceremonies. In some families, evening prayers may also be held on the days leading up to the funeral. In the lead-up to the day of the funeral, family members usually prepare food for friends and neighbours and inform visiting mourners about the cause of death of the deceased. All and sundry are expected to visit the home of the bereaved and offer their condolences. It is customary for these mourners to be served something – at least some tea and scones. Depending on the time of day, a full meal may be offered.

In her doctoral thesis, 'Mourning Rituals and Practices in Contemporary South African Townships: A Phenomenological Study', Tiny Happy Sarah Setsiba delves into the changing nature of mourning rituals among Africans. She presents traditional mourning rituals as well as prevalent contemporary practices and focuses on the phenomenon known as 'after tears'. The 'after-tears' party is held immediately after the burial of a loved one, and has become popular in black townships in South Africa. It is a vast contrast of emotions. The grieving family remains deeply sad, while the mourners turn into revellers who indulge in free-flowing alcoholic beverages. African funerals, which were once solemn and sad occasions, have been reinvented as stylishly riotous celebrations, complete with alcohol, music and dance for the black elite. Yet, despite the emergence of this alien invention of 'after tears', Setsiba insists that proper rites and ceremonies are still performed following the death of a loved one, reflecting the bereaved's strong cultural beliefs.

Any deviation from culturally specific beliefs could be perceived as a sign of disrespect for the ancestors, and bad luck could befall anyone who does not adhere to the stipulated practices. *Ngiyalwesaba ulaka lwabaphansi!* (I, for one, fear the wrath of the ancestors!) Hence, I hope against hope that I perish after I have buried both my parents.

My parents and extended family are great believers in traditional Zulu rites and ceremonies associated with the dead. These include an expectation that my wife will assume a mourning posture immediately after my death. In my culture, this means sitting in the house covered with a blanket and wearing headgear. My wife would be expected to sit next to a burning white candle with her head bowed. During the whole pre-burial mourning process she may not make any eye contact with males. She is also not expected to play any part in the funeral arrangements.

In my family's interpretation of Zulu tradition, upon confirmation of a death, there's no pre-burial mourning period. If I die in my ancestral home, I may be buried the very next day. However, if you happen to die in a hospital or in an accident, your body will be transported home on the eve of your burial. Nowadays, the burial itself may be delayed for as long as it takes for important relatives to confirm their availability. For some reason, in my family, everyone – even family members who no longer see eye to eye – bury the hatchet and attend the funeral. Most importantly, the funeral will be held on a Sunday (Saturday is the Holy Sabbath for my family). There are pre-burial rituals such as *ukuyomlanda* (going to the place where the deceased took his or her last breath) and carrying *uMlahlankosi* (the sacred tree for taking the spirit of the dead home). During the process of *ukuyomlanda*, the designated chief mourner will talk to the spirit of the dead at the scene, call the person by his or her name, and command him or her to come home. The chief mourner won't talk to anyone again on the journey until they have reached the ancestral home where the mourning process is taking place.

On the day of the funeral, a goat and a cow are slaughtered. The goat has a special function. Its bile is emptied into a basin filled with water. All the mourners wash their hands in this mixture after the burial rites have been performed. This is a cleansing ceremony to mark the separation of the dead from the living. A cow is only slaughtered if the deceased was married. According to Zulu culture (to which my family adheres), the skin of the cow is used to cover the coffin of the deceased; it is a badge of honour for the head of the family. It is now generally accepted and expected that on the day of the funeral, after the body has been lowered into the ground and the burial is over, there shall be feasting. These days, formal caterers are enlisted to prepare a three-course meal for all the mourners to thank them for their support. My family is big with these kinds of ceremonies, especially the hospitality part of the equation.

Certainly, and thankfully, there will be no 'after-tears' party for me. Both my wife and my extended family will agree on this one. The 'after tears' is a new phenomenon and happens immediately after the funeral. Friends of the deceased gather to have drinks, mostly alcoholic beverages, and they are usually in a party mood, with loud music and dance. It's a way of saying that the departed has completed his earthly role, and that those who remain should forget about him and continue with life, as Setsiba's thesis states.

According to the Mncube family tradition, immediately after my burial my wife would be expected to start the process of *ukuzila*, which involves wearing black for the duration of the *ukuzila* period. As part of the *ukuzila* period, the grieving widow must cut off all her hair. My mom explained that a goat is slaughtered for the sole purpose of obtaining ancestral permission to cut the grieving widow's hair to mark the start of the mourning season. The first nine days of the *ukuzila* period are also crucial. Of these, the first two days must be spent in seclusion. For the next seven days, the grieving widow is expected to take a bath in the early hours of the morning, before everyone else wakes up. Strangely, for all those seven long days, she is also expected not to wash her private parts. After the first nine days, the bathing regime returns to normal, but there is still an expectation that the highest levels of probity will be observed. According to my mom, during the *ukuzila* period the grieving widow must display high levels of *inhlonipho* (respect), including not talking loudly or making eye contact with men, among other things. According to my mother, the *ukuzila* period for the Mncube family has now been officially reduced to twelve months. Traditionally, it lasted for two years.

On the day of the removal of the mourning cloth to mark the end of the *ukuzila* period, a special ceremony is held. A cow and a goat are slaughtered, with the mandatory brewing of *umqombothi*. The clothes worn during the *ukuzila* period are burnt beyond recognition somewhere in the veld. The grieving widow is then presented with brand-new clothes to mark the official end of the mourning period.

A separate ceremony, known as *ukubuyisa* (returning the spirit of the dead home), is performed at the end of the mourning period. The aim of this ritual is to place the spirit of the dead in the family's kraal, where it is believed all ancestors reside. On the day of *ukubuyisa,* a branch of *uMlahlankosi* (the sacred tree for taking the spirit of the dead home) is required. The chief mourner must go to the grave of the deceased and speak to him or her. He must explain that it is now time to return home. The branch of *uMlahlankosi* must be carried from the graveyard to the family's kraal. The deceased must be informed that he has been returned home to rest with his forebears. A cow and a goat must be slaughtered for this ritual to be a success.

Dear reader, this is how I *ought* to be buried to be in line with the dictates of my Zulu culture and family traditions. But there is a snag. Firstly, my wife will not agree to a series of ceremonies to mark each burial ritual – largely because these key rituals are expensive, and because we know by now that she is averse to animal slaughter. Secondly, she won't play the grieving widow by adopting a mourning posture, sitting on a Zulu sleeping mat and going the whole hog with the *ukuzila* process.

I know my wife. She will be the chief funeral planner, meticulously ensuring that every detail is attended to. The whole funeral affair will be serene, low cost, short and swift. I know for real that she will refuse to let my body be buried in my ancestral home. And she won't be bothered with the whole shebang of observing Zulu funeral rites. She is not being difficult; it is just not her culture. She won't budge. She calls her refusal to play the Zulu cultural game a clash of values, not cultures. I am not persuaded.

Compounding the prevalent cultural stalemate is that I have no desire to be buried at all. I want my body donated to science for the furtherance of medical research and teaching. I haven't even broached the subject with my parents. They will be utterly horrified. I am told that after two to three years, the cadaver is cremated. But I want what remains of my body to be embalmed and buried in my ancestral home, without the cultural pomp and ceremony.

If wishes were horses, beggars would ride. This is our cultural quagmire, playing itself out in life and in death.

13

Marital bliss: For whom?

I wish my life mimicked my Facebook posts. On Facebook, I am rich and happily married. The truth is murkier.

My marriage is an uphill climb. In 2016, my wife blocked me on Facebook. She claimed to know nothing about it. I was trying to tag her on my status when I discovered this fact with horror. What kind of a married couple unfriends each other on Facebook? We sat together that night and befriended each other again. This episode left a bitter taste in my mouth.

However, it didn't prepare me for the catastrophe that followed. For a week, I couldn't speak to my wife on the phone. It wasn't for a lack of trying. She had been blocked on my own phone. Yes, an intruder had changed the settings and added my wife's number onto my blocked list. I have my own suspect for this treason.

As if this was not enough to cause a heart attack, my wife changed the locks in our humble abode. Yes, she didn't even hide it. In fact, she even bragged about it. She sent me an SMS: 'New lock installed on Trellidor ... So, you're locked out.' The second one was more chilling: 'Be nice and I will let you in.'

I paid no notice to these messages, well, until I got home. There she was with a smug look on her face, shouting 'You're locked out!'

Yes, indeed I was locked out. I threatened her with many things, including a divorce. She didn't care. She held all the aces.

Two weeks later, as I drove into the driveway, I almost fainted. You see, the whole exterior of our house, including the gate, is painted pink. But, on this day, the gate was black. I thought I was at the wrong house – or that I had lost my mind, but the sign said house number 405. I whipped out my cellphone to get to the bottom of this black-gate phenomenon that wouldn't open for me. My wife answered immediately. I could sense she was feeling on top of the world.

'How can I help you, Mr Mncube?' she said, clearly with a smile. I told her I thought I was lost.

She laughed hauntingly. 'Oh, I forgot to tell you the insurance paid us for the new gate. If you're nice to me, I can open it for you.'

I had learnt from my experience with the change of locks weeks earlier that threatening her with anything would get me nowhere. I promised I would be nice, a model husband. I even added that I would take the rubbish out every Wednesday without fail, and perhaps I could even relieve the pool boys. My trick worked: the black gate opened.

But she was not done with her trickery. A week later, while I was at work, she got contractors to change not just the locks, but the whole front door. Upon my arrival, I was greeted by an unfamiliar door. Thankfully, this time around I wasn't locked out, because we use the kitchen entrance for everyday use. When I asked her nicely why she didn't share all these major capital projects in our house with me, she simply smiled and kissed me.

A month after all this trickery, she proceeded to do something straight out of the movies: she took my car keys to work with her. As I was getting ready to go to work one morning, I couldn't find my keys. It never even crossed my mind that my wife might have taken them, wittingly or unwittingly. So, I combed the whole house for the missing keys with the precision of a crime-scene detective, until an hour later when Catherine, our domestic worker, mumbled something like, 'Perhaps they are in her handbag.' This took a while to sink in. Then, it hit me. My wife is capable of far worse. So, I phoned her at once. No answer. I sent numerous messages on WhatsApp – literally three messages every twenty minutes for a whole hour. No reply. It turned out that she had left her phone in her office to attend to yet another mind-numbing academic meeting.

I was too angry to speak to her when she finally picked up her cellphone. My daughter had a chat with her and reported my missing car keys. Calmly, she said, 'Oh! I have them in my handbag. I am on my way now to bring them back.'

Well, the story had a happy ending, as she stuck to her part of the bargain and returned my missing keys. It came to pass that I reported for duty at exactly 12:45 p.m.

However, on my part, I am done playing Mr Nice Guy with my wife. All I ever really wanted from her as a white person was the return of the dispossessed land. I had held back on this demand for sixteen long years. Here it is to you, Professor D.: give back the land, and all will be forgiven.

14

The bizarre case of Thabo and the Garden of Eden

I hate Thabo.

No, stupid. I am not talking about the former president, Thabo Mbeki. I am talking about our no-longer-so-new gardener. I surmise that I am, in fact, at the end of my rope with Thabo.

Ever since Thabo came into our lives three years ago, things have been going haywire. It started slowly – and probably innocently – as my wife uttered these words: 'I think Thabo is doing a good job.' Well, I guess I had to be eased into it. It then escalated into a torrential downpour. Now, the only thing on my wife's lips is Thabo this, Thabo that. I am sick and tired of it. Clearly, I am not going to hear the end of it.

As a result of Thabo's meddling with my wife's lips, my marriage is teetering on the brink of collapse. There is a prima facie case of alienation of affections. This is a legal condition that is found in common-law tort, abolished in many jurisdictions – where it still exists, an action is brought by a deserted spouse against a third party alleged to be responsible for the failure of the marriage. I am persuaded to follow a litigious course of action: to sue Thabo for loss of warmth and affection.

In my frustration, when this inadvertent flirtation began, I took to Facebook to express my outrage. Within seconds of posting about Thabo's antics, the Facebookers picked a side. I was accused of being a jealous lover. But at least one friend advised me that all Thabos are, in fact, troublesome. I believe him. Remember Thabo Mbeki and his bizarre theories about AIDS?

What I didn't know was that Thabo's stature had increased exponentially on social media since I'd posted my outrage. Before I knew it, I was getting messages from as far afield as Abu Dhabi, England and Australia. My wife travelled to Durban on business, and the first person she met asked about Thabo. Our family friends from the Eastern Cape came to visit, and the first person they asked about was – you guessed it, Thabo. It doesn't end there: even my mother-in-law has jumped on the Thabo bandwagon. So, this Thabo fellow is now a celebrity, at my expense. No dinner-table talk is complete without a legendary story of Thabo, the gardener. It seems that the Facebookers are not only intrigued about my incessant complaints about my loss of affection, but have developed a deep affection for Thabo. I now rue the day I complained about him. How I wish I could turn back the hands of time.

Anyway, last week Thabo made a fatal error. My wife reported that, upon arriving at our humble abode at 2 p.m., she found Thabo already in the changing room, changing from his work clothes to go home. I naively thought that this would be the end of Thabo. I posted as much on Facebook:

Ladies and gentlemen, countrymen and countrywomen, I am glad to report that Thabo's days are numbered. My wife – yes, she of Thabo this, Thabo that fame – caught Thabo red-handed leaving work two hours early. This is a rare opportunity for me to show that the days of disrespecting the patriarchy are over. I

must strike while the iron is hot. Thabo is to be hauled over
the coals for misconduct, conduct unbecoming of a gardener,
bringing the good name of the Mncubes' garden into disrepute,
dereliction of duty, etc.

Within seconds, Facebookers were on my case – it felt like a ton of
bricks had fallen on me. Former commissioner at the Commission
for Conciliation, Mediation and Arbitration (CCMA), Shaida Bobat,
commented: 'Thabo is forgiven on the basis of mitigating factors –
he was distressed after the US election results.' Professor Cathy
Campbell from the London School of Economics added: 'Thabo is
a lovely person and a great gardener. Am sure this was a one-off. I
agree with Shaida. The world is upside down this week.' *Sunday
Times* journalist Nivashni Nair Sukdhev commented: 'Dear Thabo.
Please contact me to do a story about your unfair dismissal.'

On Saturday, a hastily convened disciplinary hearing took place.
I guess it was my turn to make a fatal error: I was not at the hearing. My wife accorded herself the task of prosecutor as well as star
witness. After the hearing, I posted thus on Facebook:

> Ladies and gentlemen, Thabo, the sell-out, appeared before the
> DC on Saturday morning. He completely denied all the charges.
> In his defence, he says he was in the toilet, and not in the changing
> room. Since my star witness is a woman of some repute, on the
> day of the incident she didn't investigate whether the voice came
> from the toilet or the changing room.

He is off the hook, for now. Truth is, I'm at the end of my tether
with this celebrity gardener.

READERS' RESPONSES

Shaida Bobat: Professor D., hang on to Thabo. Bheki u have made me laugh so much that my tummy is sore.

Sbu Scelo Blose: He he he, why did you neglect your garden? Why do you even have a garden, even Adam was defeated by a garden?

Louise Mokonyane: Ha ha ha ha … I can't help the laughing here. Oh my gosh!

Ayanda Melansi: Commission of inquiry into Thabo's sudden popularity is needed. The garden is a dangerous place.

Angela Abrahams: Let us know how many times Thabo's name gets mentioned this evening. That could be grounds for your commission of enquiry. But remember all you ever get from those are recommendations.

Philani N. KaMakhanya: No garden of another of man shall be ploughed by another man, but only by the man himself. #caseclosed

Deborah Mindry: Too funny, but I'm with your wife, the garden is very important – keeps us sane and happy, which means it's very important to our husbands!

15

Pool Boys and Bean Boys put writer's marriage on the rocks

My wife is a flirt. Finish and *klaar*! This is not a matter of opinion, but a fact. Don't sound clever and tell me to divorce her. I won't. You see, my marriage was designed, so I thought, to be flirt-proof. In the true sense of Mills & Boon romance novels, it had – so I thought – 'that thing', so we would live happily ever after.

This was my dream: a happy marriage where I am the only one who wears the pants. Fast-forward to 2016; my dream lies in ruins after an earthquake measuring 6.9 on the Richter scale hit my marriage. The truth is, it never crossed my mind that one day I'd be having sleepless nights, worried sick about the Pool Boys and Bean Boys threatening to tear my marriage apart. I often ask myself: Is she capable of being lured into forbidden bedrooms and committing forbidden acts? Is there something about the women in my life that leads them astray? Is it me? Is it them? I don't know.

I've been mulling over this turn of events for some time now. The thought of my dearest 'young' wife cheating hit me the other day, and it's quite scary, to be honest. What worries me is not the moralistic do-not-deceive-one-another kind of stuff. The real snag here is that my wife may actually be seeing more than one guy while she is still (for lack of a better phrase) legally married to me. In fact, scratch that: seeing more than one guy in two separate groups who don't know one another from a bar of Sunlight soap.

Here is my conundrum. At first, it was the Pool Boys. Since the Pool Boys came into our lives two years ago, my marriage has become a perpetual uphill climb. Dear reader, this despite the fact that the Pool Boys have a very specific job – to keep the pool sparkling clean. I opine that the Pool Boys are playing a game of overreach. I have never been officially introduced to the Pool Boys. The big question, of course, is why they are kept a secret. There are only two reasons that make me believe that the Pool Boys exist in real life. One, of course, is that my wife keeps reminding me: 'Hey, these Pool Boys are really good. Please, come with me – let's go do pool inspection.'

She says this at least three times a week: on Tuesdays and on weekends. The second reason, of course, is that the Pool Boys get paid from my contribution to the home-maintenance budget. Out of sheer frustration, I reported my little problem with the Pool Boys to my mother-in-law. She travelled from miles away – all the way from France – to come and resolve the situation. While she was visiting, she spied on the Pool Boys. She reported back thus: 'The Pool Boys don't stand a chance. Don't worry.' I then learnt the identity of the Pool Boys – chubby, in rugged clothes, and black. I was relieved.

My sense of relief didn't last long: the Pool Boys were suddenly joined by the Bean Boys. You see, in my house we are coffee addicts. So, my resourceful wife found a coffee place in Pretoria within three hours of touching down there. For at least a year, everything went well. She would go and buy coffee beans once a week. Sometimes, she would sit at the coffee shop and do some work. I was fine with this arrangement. Well, well: voilà! The Bean Boys came out of the woodwork.

When my wife came home one day, she was full of beans. I

enquired about the cause of this sudden state of ecstasy. You guessed it: she had met the Bean Boys. She reported that the roasting method at the coffee shop had changed; as a result, the Bean Boys had given her a new roast to try out. Her excitement coupled with the words 'Bean Boys' left a bitter taste in my mouth. I knew intuitively that I was on the back foot yet again. Why would a bunch of Afrikaners give her a different roast for tasting because they had changed their roasting method? Did they extend this gesture to all customers? Why only *my* wife? Why, why, why, *Thixo wa se* George Goch? She has been going there for coffee every morning for two years. And suddenly they have taken notice of her. She is being lured into tasting some roast. Who knows what next. I must confess that the Bean Boys are urban, lean and mean. My marriage is in a downward spiral.

READERS' RESPONSES

Matebello Motloung: Hahahaha! Hai Bheki, hardly a year working for a national government department and you've become paranoid. Hahahaha! Very soon, you are going to suspect your German sedan of cheating on you.

Harri Narismulu: Hey Stalin – I see those demonic tendencies (circa Tech Natal SRC 1995) are still pervasive. If you wish to tail the ladies in your life – then that is a domestic dispute (which you will not win anyway). Now that you, in true obfuscationist-style (typical of north-of-the-river types) introduce race and ethnicity (Afrikaner, Zulu) into the mix, you drag the matter to even lower depths. Aaaah I got it – even Juju will admire your skills and will offer you a front seat next to him at the circus – sorry parly!

Rose: Do I detect a little jealousy??? Send me an air ticket and I will come over and sort out these 'bean boys' for you.

16

Sapiosexuality

Okay, let us get this one out of the way. I confess to being a sapiosexual male. If you don't know what I am on about, you're not alone. I admit to having learnt about the term only recently, yet it fits hand in glove with my character. The Urban Dictionary says a sapiosexual person is someone who finds intelligence and the human mind to be the most sexually attractive feature of the opposite sex. 'Sapiosexual' is derived from the Latin word *sapien*, which means wise or smart, and *sexualis*, which means relating to sex. It's an interesting phenomenon and a relatively new trend among the upwardly mobile middle classes.

Basically, for men like me, intellectual stimulus is the new model-like figure, complete with full, pink lips, fair skin and long legs. I have always looked, in the opposite sex, for an incisive, inquisitive, insightful and irreverent mind. Though I wouldn't go so far as to claim that I need philosophical discussion as part of foreplay. According to Dr Diana Raab, a doctor in transpersonal psychology, it is true that 'the brain can be aroused by the insights of other people. There are people who crave in-depth discussions, and they are more attracted to those who can satisfy their appetite for conversation.'

Don't call me wacky just yet. New empirical evidence is emerging that supports my sapiosexuality fetish. In a study from the University of New Mexico, Professor Geoffrey Miller asked 400 men to take an exam to test their overall intelligence. They were also asked to give a sperm sample. The study revealed that the man who had the highest score in cognitive tests had the healthiest sperm. Professor Miller concluded: 'Traits such as language, humour, and intelligence evolved in both sexes because they were sexually attractive to both sexes.'

Alpha Philea Saguiguit, a journalism graduate at the University of the East in Manila and a student of law at San Beda College, has compiled three defining traits of the sapiosexual. The first is their ability to identify intelligence in others. Sapiosexuals can pinpoint the wise man among the wise guys. They can also figure out whether the person is genuinely smart or ostentatiously smart. The second is their ability to experience an in-depth discussion about anything that interests them as the sexiest moment they could ever imagine. They also disregard looks because, for them, only intelligence is long-lasting. The third is their very good conversation skills, which make them more charming than the taciturn boy or girl next door. They usually like to share their thoughts with people who will understand them and can teach them new things. In other words, sapiosexuals are intelligent people who are more likely to end up with other sapiosexuals. I posit that my wife is a sapiosexual too. In the early days of our courtship, I remember how she engrossed herself in my earlier writing and concluded that I had a beautiful mind. For me, that was the turning point in what has become a whirlwind romantic endeavour.

In her blog, Dr Diana Raab says that being sapiosexual means that the person to whom you are attracted may also have an incisive, inquisitive and irreverent mind. As foreplay, she continues, the sapiosexual may crave philosophical, political or psychological discussions, because this turns them on. 'Those who are sapiosexual are those who are stimulated or challenged by the way another person thinks,' writes Dr Raab in a journal article published by *Psychology Today*.

To drive the point home that intellectual stimulus is the new skinny model, the University of Iowa has conducted a study every year since 1939 that asks both men and women to rank the eighteen most desirable characteristics in a long-term mate. In 1939, intelligence ranked eleventh; in 2009, it jumped to fourth, following 'mutual attraction and love', 'dependable character' and 'emotional stability'. In 2016, intelligence as the most desirable characteristic in the long-term mating game ranked number one among American men.

As you have read, I married above my intellectual station. My English wife has a PhD in sociology. When we met, she was already a senior lecturer and a PhD candidate. I found these basic facts about her completely captivating. It was bonus material for me that she had been a fervent anti-apartheid activist and human rights advocate.

These qualities fed into the traits I sought in a long-term partner. In 2000, I declared openly that I wouldn't marry any woman who did not have at least an undergraduate degree. This despite the fact that, at the time, I was an undergraduate student myself. It caused consternation among my circle of friends, who thought I was being unreasonable. Apparently, according to them, I didn't understand matters of the heart. I was told that love is blind. I stood my ground and asked them what, exactly, I would discuss with a high-school dropout or a matriculant. This has nothing to do with the financial independence that comes with a graduate and working wife or girlfriend. It went deeper: in my view, the longevity of any intimacy is driven largely by intellectual stimulation. These are historical nuggets that support my new-found view that I am, in fact, a sapio-sexual male.

However, my sapiosexuality has a long history, dating back to the 1980s. On graduating from primary school, I made a decision that there was no point in dating someone who was still in primary school. I adhered to the same principle when I graduated from high school, although it took me a full twenty-five months to start dating varsity students. It was a conscious decision not to lower the intellectual bar.

My first reciprocal love, Miss M., was a civil engineering student at the time of our romantic involvement. I vividly recall us in a passionate discussion about her favourite subject, Theory of Structures. I always found these discussions completely engrossing – more so than, say, a magazine article about yet another celebrity scandal. Today, although she is married to someone else, Miss M. holds both a diploma and a degree in civil engineering. My love life is replete with women who hold multiple higher-education qualifications.

17

I cheat, therefore I am

I am a self-confessed emotional cheat. My career in emotional cheating began by chance, when I was entangled in a love triangle a long time ago – before I married Professor D.

For me, there are two stages to any relationship. The first is the moment of awareness, of weakness (the wobbly knees), of longing to caress her, and the intrigue of letting her in on your intimate intentions. This first moment occurs even if it's not taken to its logical conclusion – dating. Inevitably, it leads to the second moment – the more 'fleshy, messy and indeterminate stuff of everyday life'. I erred on the side of caution; at the time, I had made a vow not to let my heart become entangled in the second moment.

This is how the story went. I met my partner in crime in the journalism classroom. She was a head honcho in the department, and I, a student. She was pregnant with her husband's baby. But the hormones had other ideas. She was, unwittingly, head over heels in love with me. It started slowly; I guess I had to be eased into it. At first, she would come to my second-year class just to confirm that I was in attendance. She would sneak her head in and ask, 'Is Walter in today?' I would religiously stand up and confirm my presence; she would disappear back to her office without another word. Then, she started calling me in for private engagements in her office. Our discussions were mundane, going something along these lines:

Ms J.: You're a very good student, Walter.

Me: I am trying, Ma'am.

Ms J.: Don't call me Ma'am, my name is Ms J.

Me: Yes, Ma'am. Oh God – I mean, Ms J.

Ms J.: I am worried about your Political Science 2 marks.

Me: The lecturer isn't very good.

Needless to say, the lecturer in question was fired forthwith. It escalated to a point where Ms J. would tell anybody who cared to listen just how diligent I was as a student. She went to the extent of saying I was a 'warm-hearted human being'.

'I have no doubts that, one day, Walter will a make a fine journalist,' she declared regularly to no one in particular.

At some stage, the first-year students were told to report all academic and social problems to me before rushing off to the head of department. Everybody was in awe of me. Honestly, some of the women were openly jealous that I had the ear of one of the head honchos all to myself. I was teased about my relationship with Ms J. Others were seriously affronted, because they erroneously believed that a black man was consorting with a married white woman. No one allowed the facts to get in the way. As far as everybody was concerned, Ms J. and I were dating, full stop. I must admit, though, that it did feel like I was in a secret love affair with Ms J. Every time I was with her, I felt like an emotional cheat. Truth is, I didn't love her. We didn't date, either. I liked her a lot as my lecturer. She was caring and compassionate, yet tough.

Strangely, I wasn't overly concerned that she was blurring the lines, because I knew that it was just a passing passion necessitated, in the first instance, by the raging hormones of a pregnant woman.

I was wrong. This 'love affair' continued to blossom long after she had delivered her baby. I recall how devastated she was on the day she told me about her family's decision to leave the country. She wrote her physical address down on a piece of paper and promised that, if I didn't obtain a journalism cadetship in South Africa, I was welcome to travel abroad and live with her. 'My country is booming. There are many opportunities for bright people like you, Walter,' she emphasised. I gave her a hug and promised to keep in touch.

I never did.

At the same time as the one-sided love affair with Ms J. was unfolding, I was emotionally involved with my classmate Nombuso. I say 'emotionally involved', because we weren't dating. I love dreaming, because in my dreams, she was already mine. I was completely captivated by Nombuso, but feared her rejection more than I longed for her love. In my everyday life, I was emotionally dependent on her. Everybody knew I loved Nombuso. She knew it too. I did zilch about it. Of course, she returned the favour by saying nothing. Towards the end of our studies, I heard that Nombuso had found her first love. I was devastated. My love for Nombuso was pure and emotionally charged. Yet, I allowed her the freedom to roam the streets with it. I guess Nombuso was the greatest love of my life – a love even greater for being unfulfilled.

Simultaneously, there was another woman, Miss S. She was of medium height, petite and light in complexion. She created an emotional triangle. She was in love with me but did not tell me. So I didn't know. But Miss S. was emotionally dependent on me. She telephoned me every night for a period of over a year. We would talk for at least an hour about everything under the sun except the real reason for her call. I was blind to her advances and naive to think that we were just friends. I only came to realise this the day we broke up. Yes, people who are emotionally attached to you must officially break up with you in order to move on. This move by Miss S. was necessitated by the rumour mill claiming that I was officially dating Professor D.

'Bheki, we can no longer be friends, because you're in love with a white woman.'

Miss S.'s declaration came as a shock to me. I was completely unaware of the extent of her emotional attachment to me. Nonetheless, I mumbled something like, 'It's okay, I understand.' I didn't.

There you have it: I am an emotional cheat.

18

A polyandrous relationship goes south

I have had affairs – flings, extended affairs, one-night stands, intensely carnal encounters and fantasy love affairs that never happened. My love-life story is peppered with corpses and tears.

But one story that stands tall above the rest is that of a woman named Nompilo ('she who brings life'). It turned out she was anything but. I was in a polyandrous relationship with Nompilo. No typo. Yes, you read that correctly. I was happily in love with a woman who told me on the first date that she was involved with someone else – another man. In this hierarchy of multiple sex partners (*ubufebe*), I was not what is colloquially referred to as *i-straight* or, more aptly, the main boyfriend. In Zulu, I was *isidikiselo* (the secondary lover).

In his seminal book titled *Love in the Time of AIDS*, British-born academic Dr Mark Hunter, assistant professor in the Department of Human Geography at the University of Toronto, describes these relationships in depth. He found that *i-straight* is the recognised main boyfriend. He is entitled, sometimes, to sex (no prior HIV test required) without a condom, and that entitlement extends less to *ishende* (the secret lover) and/or *isidikiselo* (the secondary lover).

My love affair with Nompilo began in earnest in about February 1995. It had taken me a full twenty-five months to date a city girl. She even received the nod as my first girlfriend to wear the pants in our relationship, literally. As a greenhorn in the city of Durban in the early 1990s, it was a novelty for me to date a woman who wore pants. Don't laugh. I am a BBT – born before technology.

Nompilo was, for the lack of a better phrase, the queen of my heart. She was beautiful – a plus-size woman of medium height and a fair complexion. So this was an accomplishment in all respects. Before I had relocated to Durban in January 1993, my intimate affairs had been taken care of by my rural pumpkins. God bless them!

During my ill-fated love affair with Nompilo, we both under-stood – or so I thought – its limits and prospects. Luckily, I was entitled to sex without a condom, even though I was the *isidikiselo*. With the benefit of hindsight, I shouldn't have taken up this benefit.

The main boyfriend, *i-straight*, was somewhere in Vryheid, in the northern part of KwaZulu-Natal. I was in Durban. The grand idea, at least in my head, was that there were clearly demarcated geographical playing fields for both of us. I would take care of Nompilo's intimate affairs in Durban, while the other guy would be a good sport and not venture into my territory. Fair play! From my side, I had no plan to see Nompilo outside the confines of the city of Durban. I had no idea that this arrangement was only a figment of my fertile imagination and would end in tears, at least for me.

However, with the benefit of hindsight, I wasn't actually in love with Nompilo, despite the fact that we had a comprehensive relation-ship. I was in love with the idea of her – she was well-spoken, well-dressed and articulate. Though our relationship stumbled from one crisis to the next, I didn't care: as long as the word was out that I had a girlfriend, I was happy.

For a start, she gifted me with a sexually transmitted disease, earning her stripes as the first woman to have done so. I demanded that she pay for my treatment. She obliged. It escalated into a series of broken promises. I let it all slide. You see, I needed Nompilo in my life to maintain some modicum of respectability. At this time, I was the deputy president of the Students' Representative Council at Technikon Natal, so a city beauty like Nompilo added an aura of respectability to my budding career in dating city girls. All was well with my soul, I thought.

Well, well, well. That was true until she nonchalantly announced, on the eve of 9 August 1995 (a Wednesday): 'My boyfriend is coming to spend the weekend at res [student residence] with me. So, I would really appreciate it if you don't cause a scene.'

I was ordered to make myself scarce.

To say I was devastated is to put it mildly. My whole world came crashing down in front of my eyes. I thought I had carved my own niche with Nompilo. In my mind, we both had a place in her heart, but I imagined that I ruled the roost in Durban. I was so naive.

On the second night of the weekend, I couldn't hold back any more. I walked the short distance to Nompilo's res. When I arrived there, it was just after midnight. I was trembling and in a cold sweat. My eyes were spitting fire. I was angry. Fuming! I stood at the door for minutes on end. Time stood still. I knew my whole world was on the other side. To deliberately misquote J.M. Coetzee from his novel *In the Heart of the Country,* 'Night falls, and Nompilo and her main boyfriend cavort in the bedroom. Hand in hand they stroke her womb.' Indeed, 'these were fair times for them'.

As I stood there, a million ways to commit the perfect murder raced through my head. At the end, a cliché won the day – if you love her enough, let her be. In the end, I didn't knock. I went back to my place and cried myself to sleep.

Thereafter, I realised the full mental and physical toll of being *isidikiselo*. It was an emotional roller-coaster ride, one for which my young, fragile heart was ill-prepared. It became clear to me that the golden cup was broken. Something inside me had died that night. I soon started the arduous journey towards breaking up with Nompilo. But I wanted the break-up to be protracted and as painful as possible. As they say, revenge is a dish best served cold.

Breaking up with Nompilo took one week and sixteen hours – a week of waiting, eight hours of planning and eight hours of execution. This is what went down. I had come to realise that I was not a priority in Nompilo's love-life. After the weekend fiasco, I pretended that all was well. So, during the week I invited her for a sleepover that weekend. I knew very well that she was bound to falter. At the last minute, she changed the plan, telling me that she was visiting some friends in Umlazi. I just knew she was lying.

So, on the Saturday, I booked the SRC shag-wagon, aka Microbus, and my friend drove me to Nompilo's flat. Surprise, surprise! Nompilo was there, not in Umlazi. Petulant, I refused to speak to her – because she was not there, in my mind, as per her phone call to me. I took a seat in her flat and started chatting away with the two friends with whom she shared the flat. After what amounted to hours of small talk, I announced that I was leaving, without having said a word to Nompilo. Nompilo's friends did not know the full story, or what was going through my mind. As I was closing the door, they insisted that Nompilo at least accompany me to the car. She agreed to come with me. Big mistake – she played right into my hands.

I ushered her into the car and instructed the driver to get a move-on. You see, I had made a pact with my driver friend – he would drive me to Nompilo's flat and later get a chance to go see his girlfriend. I had no desire to tamper with this deal. It suited me just fine. My friend drove to Point, in downtown Durban. When he left, I said he must not worry about us, as we were not in a hurry. He was gone for maybe five hours. I never said a word to Nompilo for those five hours. When my friend came back, I instructed him to drive us to Corlo Court residence, my flat. Upon our arrival, I told him he could take the car for the night, as I wouldn't have any need for it. This despite the fact that I knew Nompilo would need a lift back to her flat. I didn't care. I signalled to Nompilo to get out. I sat her down in my flat and recounted all her lies, half-truths and broken promises; after about four hours of ranting, I told her to get out of my room and never come back. She left in crocodile tears.

Anyway, she had to go. She had outlived her usefulness in my life. She had become a burden that was too great to bear. Loving Nompilo was emotionally exhausting. At first, it was new and exciting. My first girlfriend to wear pants – yes, at one stage this was a novelty. The first woman to give me an STI – yes, she gave me more than I bargained for, not once but twice. At least she forced me to consider regular condom use.

You may ask how I know she gave me the STI. Don't be stupid: she happened to be my first and only girlfriend in Durban. You guys don't understand – you may be a hit in your rural village, but urban (Durban) girls are something else.

READERS' RESPONSES

Thulani Msimang: It would be funny if it wasn't so sad. Chin up mate.

Noloyiso Mtembu: At least she had the decency to warn you. Guys who do the same thing just disappear or double book themselves and when you show up they act all surprised. And as a woman you're supposed to accept that 'men do this all the time'. Hardy for the heartache ?? welcome to most women's love story.

Ndumiso Mapholoba Ngcobo: *Umuntu akumele athi eyinyoni bese eba yisigwadi.* It's important to pick one battle and fight it.

Nombuso MaMshengu Shabalala: Hahahaha so you were a hit *emafamu angakini, uNompilo wakushintsha konke lokho wakufundisa iTheku*!! Hehehehe sorry about the breakup.

Ayanda Melansi: Look Nompilo has no intention of living up to her name. She strikes me as a person who does the total opposite. Well Mr Mncube *wazisiza wadla phansi*.

Nivashni Nair Sukdhev: Bullshit! Today is a reminder of how you could have lost the true love of your life and happiness. If you stayed with her you wouldn't have met the most amazing woman and had the blessing we call Miss N. Now suck it up and get real!

19

Cebisile

Today I confess I was once a ladies' man. That's right: I was a
Casanova of note in my heyday. I have been involved in many
'casual relationships' – from Zodwa, the love of my life, greater for
being unfulfilled, to Busi, the terrible kisser, to Nompilo, and to
Thule, my yellow-bone, a village beauty and snazzy dresser who
died prematurely.

Of all my 'casual relationships', one stands out. I had something
special with my close-friend-turned-lover, Cebisile ('the one who
helps with a good idea'). In the modern parlance, my relationship
with Cebisile could be described as friends with benefits.

Cebisile and I knew that we were in a 'casual relationship'. I was
free to date other women. I guess she was free to date someone else
too, if she wanted. But she chose me, warts and all.

Psychologists have long warned that true love and commitment
are a rare find. They insist that, many times, romantic relationships
are not based on love at all, but are casual and sexual in nature. I
know many a girl who would scoff at the idea of a 'casual relationship', choosing, rather, to live with the delusional white lie that their
relationships are more formal romantic relationships. Cebisile and
I had no delusions of grandeur.

Cebisile was short, and always full of beans. It was this natural cheerfulness that drew me to her. She was a charmer extraordinaire. Cebisile's presence in my life did wonders for my ego. Yet she wasn't my ideal girlfriend, as I preferred them tall, slender and yellow-boned. But Cebisile was cut from a different cloth; she had that thing. To borrow from the Songs of Solomon, Cebisile had dove's eyes, teeth like a flock of shorn sheep and lips like a strand of scarlet. I wouldn't say I was head over heels in love with Cebisile. Nonetheless, we had a comprehensive romantic relationship – except we never had sex.

Yes, you read that right. No sex – full stop. A Casanova was involved in a sexless casual relationship. Sex therapists agree with me that sex is important in a relationship. They say sex means so much more than just getting our rocks off. 'It's a way to connect, show love, develop trust, be vulnerable, be authentic, or soothe each other,' says Vanessa Marin, a sex therapist based in San Francisco. Yet here I was with a hot young thingy and couldn't get it on. It wasn't hormonal – Cebisile's libido was in full throttle, and it wasn't that I suddenly had lower than normal testosterone levels. I was hot-blooded, like all other philanderers. Truth is, we made a vow of sexual abstinence. This had nothing to do with religious reasons. I had no idea why a woman in her twenties would say no to sex, but yes to a relationship with a known womaniser.

Although I was puzzled by her no-sex stance, I played along, largely because I valued my friendship with her. I must admit, I wanted more.

I would be telling a lie if I said I was looking forward to Cebisile's first sleepover at my humble abode. But, oh boy! I should have. Cebisile gave me free lessons in sexual pleasure without going all the way. After our first carnal encounter, I almost fell in love with her. Of all my casual relationships that year, the one I had with Cebisile was second to none.

I spent a lot of quality time with Cebisile, until we lost contact. The last time I saw her was late in 1998. She was still gentle, but frail. We exchanged telephone numbers again and agreed to meet to rekindle the flames of our 'love' affair. We never did.

I only learnt about Cebisile's death in mid-2000. I was going through my old diaries when I chanced upon her landline number. I dialled the number; the voice on the end of the line said, 'Let me call an adult.' I knew something big had happened to my dearest Cebisile. The elder squandered no time. She simply announced that Cebisile had died and had been buried the previous year.

Why am I telling you this story? Wait. I learnt later from other family members that Cebisile had died as a result of AIDS-related conditions.

Cebisile was my soul mate. I am grateful to her for protecting me and loving me completely, to the detriment of her own happiness. She put her whole being into the service of those like me, who, at the time, were ignorant about the virulent HIV/AIDS epidemic. In the mid-1990s, some of us knew very little about protecting ourselves against HIV. We used condoms intermittently, and there were no antiretroviral drugs to slow the spread of the disease once infected. The only method that truly worked was abstinence.

To this day, I salute Cebisile for loving me enough to want me to live an HIV/AIDS-free life. May her sweet and gentle soul rest in peace!

READERS' RESPONSES

Gafieldien Benjamin: That is selflessness. She was a selfless person. Only someone respecting others and caring so much about others can be called selfless. I hope she rests in peace. Happy Women's Day to you Cebisile, wherever you are.

Doreen Gough: Wow – what a story! Very touching.

Thozama La-Reina UmaMbili: She probably thought to herself, 'Let me enjoy this young man's great company before this life-threatening disease sends me back to my Maker.' *Siyabonga ngabantu abanjengaye.* We hope she is resting in peace.

Baartman Anne: This was a caring woman … may her good soul rest in peace …

Nkosinathi Mzwamahlubi Myataza: This is so deep brother! Touching! May her beautiful soul rest in peace!

20

Valentine's Day: Fourteen roses and a funeral

I admit it: I am a hopeless romantic. Several years ago, I bought fourteen roses for Thule as a surprise gift for Valentine's Day. I was prepared to go the whole hog, complete with candlelight dinner, French champagne and sweet jazz music. She never received the roses. I never got to see her. She had left town hurriedly, for good.

Thule was my kind of girl. She was tall, like a model, slender but not skinny, and light in complexion – a true yellow-bone. She had everything going for her – a perfect body complete with curves. She had beautiful blue eyes, and a set of dazzling, angel-white teeth. She had sweet lips, soft as blossoms, that spoke only words of kindness, a soothing voice and a bubbly personality. When she smiled, she lit up the room. Her high cheekbones made her face almost perfect. She permanently smelled good – the scent of her perfume always mesmerised my senses. When she walked, it looked like a perfectly choreographed movement. She spoke softly, with her iconic smile permanently on.

It didn't help that she was a hairstylist by profession and ran her own hair salon. She always wore her hair long and in some sophisti-cated, darkie kind of way. And she dressed to kill, always wearing different gold chains around her neck. I enquired once about her sense of fashion; she said, 'I design my own clothes.'

Thule was a true village beauty, beautiful inside and out. I was head over heels in love with her. She had ravished my heart. She was always on my mind. In my downtime, I imagined her soft lips touching mine and whispering sweet nothings into my ear. She was indeed my lily flower.

Our love for each other was reciprocal. She boosted my ego no end. She always remarked that my smile was infectious, and told me I wasn't capable of making her angry. She was into it as much as I was. With her, it had been love at first sight. I didn't know that this was possible. So, why had she left town unexpectedly? I guess I will never know.

Dear reader, let me take you back to midday on that fateful Valentine's Day. I was dressed to the nines. I had fourteen roses in my hands. I was high on love. As I walked up the stairs into Thule's hair salon, I was humming the melody of Don Williams's 'True Love', which is hard to find and even harder to keep.

I entered the salon only to be met by sombre faces. Thule was nowhere in sight; three of her friends, who were styling clients' hair, stopped in their tracks when they saw me. I couldn't understand why the women who had always been happy to see me had had such a change of heart. There was sudden pandemonium as the girls spoke among themselves, trying to figure out who was the eldest. I was bamboozled.

A hastily convened caucus agreed on the representative who would speak to me. The chosen one didn't hesitate. She announced the news matter-of-factly – Thule was dead. She was buried last month. The words cut deep into my heart. Fortunately, they allowed the words to sink in properly before they started weeping in unison – crying no longer for Thule, but for me.

Time stood still. This was a moment of reckoning for me: for more than a month, I had neither phoned nor seen the woman with whom I told anyone who cared to listen that I was in love. There was no cogent reason for this lack of communication. I had last seen her in late December. She had mentioned that she wasn't feeling well. I had advised her to seek medical help. We parted on good terms. I planted a kiss on her forehead, and promised to see her in the new year. The Valentine's Day appearance with fourteen roses was meant to atone for my lack of communication and reignite the fire between us. Well, well ... the woman I wanted to surprise had a bombshell waiting for *me*. As my shock subsided, grief set in. Tears started rolling down my cheeks. My lily flower had died an agonising death. Alone, and lonely.

It was many moons ago, but it still hurts deeply. I didn't have a chance to say goodbye. None of her friends had my cellphone number, so nobody had informed me of the sad news.

I was so devastated that I threatened to mourn for her publicly by wearing black mourning cloth. I never did. I left, the fourteen roses still in my hand. I have no recollection of what I did with them.

Yes, I have loved and been loved by the best. Goodbye, my lily flower. We shall meet in paradise. I will bring roses with me.

21

Zodwa: My first, and greatest, love

At the tender age of nine, I fell in love for real. As you know, the object of my desire was my classmate Zodwa. She was tall, slim, light in complexion and extraordinarily beautiful. She exuded class and confidence. There was a sparkle in her eyes. I was mesmerised by her mere presence. Zodwa's voice was kind and sounded musical to my ears. She had a self-effacing demeanour about her. Clearly, I was intensely in love with her.

I had found my true love in Zodwa, whatever that means when you're in lower primary school. I spent the first five years after having met her (if you could call it that) stealing glances at her. Every time the teacher left the classroom, or during those lovely things called free periods, I would move from my desk and position myself where I would have a better view of her. I would stare at her for minutes on end. However, any accidental eye contact would make me swing my head away faster than Usain Bolt.

For five long years, I never said a word to her. It wasn't for lack of trying. Words just escaped me – and I couldn't bear the thought of not being in love with her if she were to say no. So, I decided it was better for this love affair to be a one-way-street kind of love. This suited me just fine. Okay, most parts of this paragraph aren't true. I wanted Zodwa in my arms. I wanted to spend the rest of my life with her. I wanted her all to myself, and to myself alone. Don't ask me what I was going to do with her, because frankly I did not know. Don't judge me; I am trying to tell a love story here.

At some stage, when I was in Standard 4, I devised what I thought was a perfect plan: Zodwa would be separated from her friends, which would result in an accidental meeting between the two of us – just me and her. It was a simple plan. It went like this: after the class prefect had decided on the cleaning-duty roster for the week and pasted it on the wall, I would sneak back to the classroom after school and change it. The grand idea was that she would be left behind for classroom cleaning, allowing for a perfect accidental meeting. I would also let my friends leave without me. As soon as everyone had disappeared, barring the cleaning crew, I would do a recce to satisfy myself that all was clear. I would then leave the school and hide in the bushes a few metres away. There, I would wait in anticipation. The time spent waiting would not be wasted, as I could practise my lines. I would say something like, '*Hawu Zodwa, yini uhambe wedwa namhlamnje? Ngicela uku-kuphelezela?* (Why are you on your own today? May I accompany you home?)'

The thing is, Zodwa was a smart girl. As soon as I emerged from the bushes, she would probably speak first. '*Hey we-Walter, uyazi uMama wakho ukuthi ula?* (Hey, Walter, does your mom know you're still here?)'

I would mumble something while my heart pumped faster and faster and I sweated as though it was raining inside my shirt. I would immediately lose my voice. Before I had time to recover, Zodwa would be a kilometre away on her own. Ja, right. Perfect plan, my foot! The scene outlined here replayed itself over and over in my mind until we finished primary school.

In high school, although my confidence was up and I still hoped to lay my hands on Zodwa, somehow it never happened. It seems she grew up faster than me: suddenly, she had a boyfriend. I was devastated. Nonetheless, we were good friends. I still loved her, yet no formal approach was ever made. I was consumed by fear of the unknown.

By the time we finished high school, she had dated maybe ten different guys. There were rumours that she had already had four abortions by the time we completed matric. I will never know the truth; those rumours may have been spread by jealous and jilted lovers.

After matric, I lost contact with Zodwa. I bumped into her only once, in 1999, at the Eshowe taxi rank while I was visiting some friends. She was a changed woman. She was darker, and the glint of beauty in her eyes had disappeared. She looked like any other ordinary girl. I later learnt that she had contracted the deadly virus, HIV/AIDS.

In a *Witness/Echo* column published in 2003, I wrote thus about Zodwa: 'It is now history that I never got closer to Zodwa. Today, Zodwa is part of our new breed of celebrities, popularly known as people living with HIV. She has been living with HIV for eight years. Her two children died recently as a result of HIV/AIDS. Unlike many other people living with HIV, Zodwa was not raped. She had sex with a variety of partners and, in the process, contracted the disease.'

In 2013, when I went to Eshowe to bury a half-sister who had died of AIDS, I enquired about Zodwa's whereabouts. Sadly, I was told to look into the majestic mountains of Mpehlela: 'Lower your eyes until you spot a white tombstone – that's Zodwa's grave.' Zodwa had died a few years after our last, chance encounter. Goodbye, Zodwa. I shall forever love and miss you.

READERS' RESPONSES

Smah Collin: I have just read this piece and it's a wow!!! You have great writing skills. SA lacks and is in need of black writers. So I am encouraging you to put your gloves on and do this. You're already a few steps closer. You will be proud at the end and you won't be the only one nathi as your fellow blacks *sobe sikujabulela* … (as fellow blacks we would be happy for you).

Bheki Mbanjwa: Once published I will be among the first to buy it!!! Damn! I will queue all night if I have to, with the hope that the book will shed some light on a few things that continue to baffle me, including … your sudden departure from Willies Mchunu's office at Transport.

Silindelo Nicholas Gwabini: Such material is always worth publishing for the next generation to read it and one day they will say I first read this chapter on my Facebook wall.

Khosi Biyela: Wow! This is interesting, go on … #patientlywaiting

Mthunzi Mnyamana Gumede: Loser! Once you publish a book, I will buy one extra copy and dedicate it to Zodwa.

Thabang T-Ba'g Chiloane: I admire your style of writing.

22

Ria: Fantasy and rites of desire

Ria was a softly spoken and unassuming white Afrikaner woman who was imbued with the triple Bs: brawn, brain and beauty. My memory is hazy as to whether Ria was a perfect picture of a beautiful white woman, complete with blonde hair and blue eyes. All I recall is that she was a brave soul, kind-spirited and courageous. She represented a generation of white people who shouted from the rooftops that apartheid was 'not in my name'. She told everyone who cared to listen that it was time to organise for freedom. She relinquished the privileges of her white race to join the anti-apartheid movement, risking the ire of her right-wing parents. In the process, she strayed from the *volk* and its political project of protecting the Afrikaner national identity and promoting white supremacy. Instead, she swapped 'her people' for 'the people'. Ria's political journey was fraught with peril, even though we were in the penultimate stages of white supremacist rule.

Despite her self-effacing demeanour, she was a giant to me. She was an exemplar of probity, selflessness and courage. When many a comrade was beginning to sink into despondency as a result of heightened political violence, Ria offered hope, resilience and intellectual clarity. She was the moral conscience of our struggle against apartheid. If she was still in it despite her parents' right-wing politics, and despite burying comrades every week, I had to stay in it too. For her, the political upheaval of the time was a sign that apartheid as a system was unworkable. All it needed was one last push. We, our generation, both black and white, had a moral duty to bring the apartheid flag down both physically and metaphorically. At Technikon Natal, we *did* bring the apartheid flag down physically. We organised a march and burnt every apartheid flag in sight. I remember clearly that those flags were never replaced; on the morning of 28 April 1994, the flag of the new South Africa took its rightful place across campus. But I digress.

Ria was a woman – a beautiful woman, and an intelligent woman at that. You couldn't help but fall in love with her. Her feisty political stance was a huge turn-on for many a male comrade. As a sapiosexual male, I immediately fell in love with her intelligence, political consciousness and clarity of mind. This was the beginning of the most beautiful and fulfilling relationship I ever had during that period.

It didn't help that we clicked immediately and became more than just political comrades, but friends. I spent a substantial amount of time in her flat at Durban's Berea Centre, and she spent a considerable amount of time on campus hanging out with me. We talked about everything under the sun, but our preoccupation was always about the state of students' organisations and anti-apartheid politics, the role of alternative media and, of course, the nirvana that would be post-apartheid South Africa. Not for a minute did we doubt that the dawn of freedom was nigh. We were eternal optimists.

We really enjoyed each other's company. I even learnt to hug – a proper hug, with a self-delaying mechanism for maximum effect. Those hugs marked an end of racial division and the birth of a new country in my head long before the new flag was hoisted at the Union Buildings one minute after midnight on Wednesday 27 April 1994. I miss those hugs – they were always a serene moment for reflection on what was, indeed, possible in the land of our birth.

The first time I met Ria is still ingrained in my mind. It is still a pulsating, living memory inside me. We were introduced by a mutual comrade, the late Comrade Derrick Anderson. We quickly realised that we were from the same town, Eshowe. Given the politics of the time, it was natural that she came from a different part of the town. She was from the part of Eshowe that was 'blessed with abundant natural diversity', the part where residents boasted that 'there was a flower in a tree every day of the year', where the environment was lush and the climate refreshing. Me, I came from the rural hinterland, barren land meant only for black people according to the Group Areas Act. As I've written, there was absolutely nothing lush about my village. We had no running water, tarred roads or electricity. Nonetheless, Ria and I called each other 'homeboy' and 'homegirl'.

We met as equals in the city of Durban. We were both hot-headed anti-apartheid activists. But the commonality between us went beyond politics and geography. We wanted an end to the apartheid regime. We dreamed of a country where black and white could live together, side by side, and succeed in the country of their birth through effort, rather than the accident of their birth. Dreamers, indeed. But I am getting ahead of myself.

Dear reader, let me take you back to the beginning. This is how the story of my fantasy affair with Ria unfolded. I met Ria in the early 1990s, while she was a student at the University of Natal (now the University of KwaZulu-Natal). She was most probably in her twenties. It was a rare fit for an Afrikaner woman from the platteland to be fully conscious of the apartheid regime's machinations and have a desire to fight for a non-racial, non-sexist and democratic South Africa. She was ahead of her time, a trailblazer of note – more so because this was after the National Union of South African Students (NUSAS) days. NUSAS was an organisation aimed at representing and promoting the interests of university and college students. It was open to students of all races, but it was predominantly white. It morphed into a serious anti-apartheid formation, pushing for universal franchise. In 1991, it merged with other student movements to form the South African Students' Congress (SASCO). The establishment of SASCO answered questions about whether it was possible to establish a single, non-racial, progressive student organisation in tertiary education institutions. SASCO is still the leading student organisation in tertiary institutions, with the bulk of SRCs in the country under its leadership. Critical interventions, such as the formation of the National Student Financial Aid Scheme (NSFAS), and a continuing battle to increase the sustained participation of poor students in the higher-education landscape are some of the credits the organisation can claim.

Ria became my political sparring partner in the anti-apartheid movement, especially the South African Students' Press Union (SASPU). SASPU was established in 1977 as an umbrella body of student newspapers and radio stations on tertiary campuses. It sought to promote vibrant student media in South Africa. Many progressive journalists and leaders of the media and communications industry of today are products of SASPU. At the time, I was the media officer of the Technikon Natal SRC. Ria's preoccupation was with the production of alternative media products to ignite students' progressive political consciousness. At some stage, I served with her on the SASPU KwaZulu-Natal Regional Executive Committee. I served a full term as regional political education officer. Of all the anti-apartheid organisations that I served, SASPU provided me with something akin to a spiritual home. Yes, it was predominantly white, but that didn't matter. We were in it together to change the lives of students and broader society through alternative and independent media.

We had been working together for just over a year when the idea that Ria might become my girlfriend took me by surprise. There was something melodramatic about it. It was sudden and passionate. There was even something revolutionary about it. It hit me where it hurt the most: my heart. I guess, for a while, Ria was an object of my desire. When she was only that, I dismissed it as something physical and sexual. I blamed it on raging hormones. As they say, poor hormones never get good press.

But when it became clear that the beast of the apartheid regime was crumbling, I became preoccupied with the type and nature of the post-apartheid family. Ria fit my prototype of a girlfriend – brainy, political and beautiful. And yes, a white Afrikaner to boot. To me, it made absolute sense to marry outside my race in a last-ditch effort to live the dream of a non-racial South Africa. So, my love for Ria was emotional, political and psychological. There was something inside me – something well beyond the moment of weakness and wobbly knees – that knew Ria was the one, the love of my life. The feelings I had for Ria were similar to what I felt as a nine-year-old entangled in an emotional fantasy love affair with Zodwa.

Liberation, to me, meant remaking individuals in the image of a new country. It wasn't only about the rebirth of the country, but of its citizens, too. Falling in love with a daughter of my former oppressor was, in itself, ground-breaking. I imagined my love affair as something equivalent to falling in love with God. There was something about it that went beyond physical and emotional attachments – something that would lead to the praxis of justice served. I imagined that, if – truly – the political gods were on our side in the new South Africa, Ria would be on my side, and mine alone. Yes, we would marry, buy a big house in the formerly white suburbs and fill it with children. And live happily ever after.

That was my dream: a humble dream to start a family line separate from that of my father.

But Ria was my friend and a true comrade. I didn't even know how to broach the subject of reorganising our relationship into something more personal and, possibly, physical. At the back of my mind I feared that Ria would be furious with me and assume that I was taking advantage of her friendly nature. Anyway, I grappled with the political question of how we were going to relate to each other after the declaration of love if she rejected my advances. My love for Ria was just too precious to be sullied by rejection. In fact, my greatest fear was the *moment* of rejection. In the end, as a disciplined cadre of the movement, I sacrificed my happiness for the greater good. I never broached the subject with her. It remained just that – a fantasy love affair. Despite that, my love for Ria was genuine. Like my love for Zodwa, it was greater for being unfulfilled.

Most students on campus assumed that the white girl who was always hanging around Walter was, well, his girlfriend. I wouldn't in a million years have confirmed or denied such rumours. The situation suited me just fine. So I was sort-of together with Ria for three years. And it didn't help that Ria's friend – another white girl – was dating a black guy.

But there was more to Ria than just a fantasy love affair. Perhaps the abiding memory of my relationship with her is what she taught me: selflessness, courage and higher ethics. I learnt a lot from my political relationship with her, including what sounded, at the time, like a strange concept: non-homophobia. She explained that people had different sexual orientations. These people included those who consider themselves lesbian, gay, bisexual, transgender and intersex (LGBTI). She said that any discrimination against these people was not only irrational, but went against the principles that underlie the new society we sought to build on the ashes of apartheid. It took me a while to understand this. I knew only of gay people at the time. I always thought they were a bit strange, but I never thought I should exclude or discriminate against them. Ria told me that this was not enough: we had to fight for them to enjoy the same rights as heterosexuals. Wow! So, that's how it came to pass that, when one of my confidantes disclosed to me that he was gay, I was, like, okay – cool, dude.

In my time with Ria, I also learnt about the power of the media. To Ria, the importance of freedom of expression – including freedom of the media – was sacrosanct. She placed a particular premium on alternative media forms to avoid the agenda-setting that character-ised the private interests of the big media conglomerates. She was for grassroots-inspired alternative media.

I drank from the well of her wisdom. It came to pass that Ria was the editor of my first attempt at publishing a newsletter. Today, as a seasoned media professional, I can safely say I am a product of SASPU – and, by extension, of Ria.

23

True love, true betrayal and a baby boy

When I broke up with my first true reciprocal love, my whole world came crashing down. It is the only break-up on record that drove me to taking up smoking cigarettes again. I had stopped smoking because my first true love, Miss M., had commanded me to quit. It was par for the course that, for as long as I was dating her, I wouldn't smoke.

Certainly, Miss M. was my kind of girl – petite, tall and light in complexion. When I broke up with her, it hurt so badly that I thought I would never recover from the heartache. I hated the sunshine, the sunrise and, yes, the sunset too. I hated life itself. I missed everything about her – her perfume, her gentle smile and her general demeanour.

The break-up was acrimonious, messy and heartbreaking. At its core was a mixture of immaturity, jealousy and alleged infidelity (on her part). Of course, nobody said anything about my own shenanigans while I was dating Miss M. With benefit of hindsight, perhaps the break-up shouldn't have happened. It occurred dramatically after I learnt that she had visited an ex-boyfriend one weekend. I didn't get to know the full story, but for me something broke that day.

There was no turning back, despite the fact that I was deeply in love with her. She was my first real reciprocal love. She may not have known how deeply I had invested my emotions in our relationship.

Compounding the situation was that, at the time of our relationship, I was a broken man. My life was spiralling out of control. My position as SRC president was precarious at best. And my life was in danger from the Concerned Group of Students. As a result, I had full-time armed bodyguards lurking in the background. I had effectively stopped attending any academic classes and retreated to my flat – reading novels and playing love songs. Simultaneously, I had been diagnosed with major depressive disorder, or clinical depression. I was receiving no treatment. As far as I was concerned, my life had hit a cul-de-sac. Miss M. had no knowledge of my real situation. On the surface, all looked well.

Nonetheless, it is a pedantic detail that, at the time of the breakup, she was pregnant and I didn't know about it. It is neither here nor there that I actually initiated the break-up. I specifically told her over the phone never to speak to me or come see me again. It is also irrelevant that the allegations of infidelity were never proven. I guess it is also a moot point that there were many feeble attempts at reconciliation after I learnt about her pregnancy. All these came to nought. The sticking point was that I wanted Miss M. to pronounce that the unborn baby was mine, and not the other guy's she was allegedly seeing. She reasoned that I was being impossible. In her mind, I should have accepted responsibility – 'manned up', as it were.

It became clear to me that she had taken the break-up badly and couldn't handle my anger and suspicion. This unresolved anger and desperation led her to make what I consider, to this day, to have been a terrible decision. She decided she would raise the unborn baby on her own.

All the same, I loved Miss M. In fact, I loved her long after our break-up. I told anyone who cared to listen that I would marry Miss M. one day. It never happened; life happened instead.

She gave birth to my firstborn all by herself. I didn't even know the due date. I never had any proof that the child existed – until that life-changing moment on an ordinary afternoon when I met my baby boy for the very first time, by accident, in the Musgrave shopping mall in Durban, that is. He was four years old. It was an emotional moment. To rub salt into the wound, he didn't even know that I was his real father. I had no right to hold my own son and kiss him. As I spoke to his mom, he tightened his grip on the man who was holding his hand. He may have been scared of meeting a stranger and was being held by another man – a man unfamiliar to me. It hurt deeply that my son was being raised by a random stranger.

All my life, I had believed in the saying that there has been no greater villain in the story of mankind than the bad father. Of course, I knew this only too well. I had been raised by an abusive father who had verbal tantrums and physically abused my siblings. He would shout profanities at the slightest provocation and ruled by fear. He would humiliate through unprintable words both the child and his wife in one sentence. And he showed no affection towards his wife or children. He was truly a monster.

For four long years, before the chance encounter with my son, I feared becoming the man I hated – my father. He had children scattered all over the place, though he paid no attention to them. To him, children were a necessary nuisance that could be ignored. I speak about my father in the past tense, because in my world he doesn't exist.

Deep in my heart, I have always known that I am not my father. I had a dream of a family that was unlike his. My dream was to start a new family line, a humble line of my own running parallel to my father's line. I envisioned a house full of sons – yes, I only wanted boy children. I wanted my new family line to continue to infinity. As J.M. Coetzee writes in his novel *In the Heart of the Country*, I imagined that my first son would be the obedient one who would stay at home and be a pillar of support, who would marry a good girl and continue the family line.

I am glad I lived to tell these tales. Of course, I have a wonderful and handsome son, but there is a twist to my dream family – I also have a girl child, whom I love dearly.

24

The challenge of pleasure: Re-imagining sexuality and consent

I may not be a rapist, but I almost crossed the line once. I slept with my first girlfriend without discussing the matter of consent. This episode in my life has left a bittersweet memory.

You may ask whether re-imagining sexuality and consent has anything to do with my advancing years or the rise of black feminism. The answer is no. All I am yearning for is to clear my conscience, and start afresh as a new man. The burden of the past is too much to bear.

I take ownership of this sad chapter in my life, despite the fact that the act itself was not rape per se. I grew up in a community that perpetuated misogynistic behaviours, and a patriarchal upbringing was the norm. I guess it is also neither here nor there that I was too immature to form criminal intent. Equally, it is a pedantic detail that she and I continued dating long after the sad episode.

In my adult (mature) view, if someone, at any point, commits an act of aggression – albeit covertly – against a girlfriend, or anybody, the resultant sexual encounter may not be consensual in a legal sense of the word. I know some 'clever blacks' would ask: Did she say no at any stage? The rhetorical question would be: Did I request her consent at any stage? Of course, the elephant in the room is that I never did. Was I naive? Perhaps. But, in all honesty, all I recall is that, at the back of our young minds, we were hell-bent on getting laid that night, by hook or by crook. Thank God, it wasn't by crook. There was implied consent evidenced by a reciprocal show of affection.

According to my diary, the now-torn exercise book that recorded the major events in my life between 1989 and 1993, my first girlfriend was Nokwazi. My diary entry records the event thus: '1991 July 15, "coronation" day by Nokwazi'. A coronation is usually quite glitzy and full of pomp. However, in my 'hood, if you had a new girlfriend in those days, colloquially speaking you would say, '*Ingicrownile leya cherry izolo.*' Literally translated, this means 'that girl crowned me yesterday'. So, all diary entries about new girlfriends simply record the event as 'coronation day'.

Nokwazi was not my dream girl. She was slim, dark and short. She did not exude confidence or class. She was just a normal country bumpkin. I just so happened to have had the guts to say the magic words – 'I love you' – and, naive as she was, she just fell in with me. Nonetheless, I must say this event of obtaining my first girlfriend was indeed widely celebrated.

Nokwazi was from a neighbouring village known as Gawozi. With my newly found love, I adopted a new habit: writing love letters. I must have written five letters a week to Nokwazi over the two years that our loveless relationship lasted. Our face-to-face visits were a rarity, however.

At some point in 1991, we received intelligence from our mutual friend (a woman) that Nokwazi and my brother's girlfriend had been granted a night-out pass to attend a function in their neighbourhood. Our mutual friend suggested that we attend it too. This presented a perfect chance for us to get laid.

We got so excited that meticulous, military-style planning began immediately. On the day in question, we left home at about 3 p.m., armed with heavy jackets and concealed okapi knives. The grand idea was that, if the girls refused to accompany us home, we were going to scare them. We had no intention of using force. Our journey lasted an hour on foot.

Sadly, Nokwazi and her friend had no idea that we were coming or that their virginity was in jeopardy. We took our position on the hill overlooking Nokwazi's homestead so that we could monitor all her movements, which we did until sunset. At this point, we needed better intelligence, as we could no longer rely on daylight. So, we contacted our mutual friend. She promised that the function would start at 8 p.m. There was already an agreement among the girls – our mutual friend, Nokwazi and my brother's girlfriend – that all of them were going to attend the function. So, we waited. Our waiting was not in vain.

At about 10 p.m., our mutual friend delivered our girlfriends on a platter. Although we were in a mean mood by then, we were mellowed by their presence. We announced that we were all going to sleep at the Mncubes that night. The matter was non-negotiable. So, we pleaded for maximum co-operation. They were stunned.

Nonetheless, they started co-operating immediately, by walking the talk towards the Mncube household some eight kilometres away. We got there at about midnight and had our way with the girls. In the morning, we patted ourselves on the back for a job well done.

After the night of the long knives, the girls were released at the crack of dawn and only accompanied halfway to their destination. They left with their virginity and dignity in tatters. Despite the fact that there was neither resistance from the girls nor any force used, I am not persuaded that we didn't rob them of their prized personal purity, honour and worth. In today's constitutional democracies, it may be considered a violation, all in the name of love. It still feels like it was wrong, on many different levels. I have not been able to escape feeling guilty, as I may have forced myself on a defenceless woman. However, the evidence suggests that, at the time, it was considered normal to proceed on the basis of non-verbal communication.

Even though our love affair flourished for quite some time after this sad chapter, to Nokwazi and all young women who have suffered a similar fate, I apologise from the bottom of my heart. I now know better.

25

Busi: Toxic masculinity and gender-based violence

I confess to once having lost my cool with a woman. Until that point, I had considered myself to be cool, calm and rational. I have no cogent defence for my repugnant action. My toxic patriarchal upbringing had a lot to do with the way we viewed women in apartheid South Africa. The woman at the receiving end of my misogyny-fuelled anger was Busi. We were in a romantic relationship, in spite of the fact that Busi was a terrible kisser. But that's not the reason she got on the wrong side of my anger.

To use J.M. Coetzee's words, Busi was a 'big-boned voluptuous feline woman'. I wouldn't go so far as saying that I loved her. She came into my life at a time when it was fashionable to have multiple and concurrent sexual partners, all in an effort to fit in. My diary entry records the actual onset of our loveless relationship as 21 April 1992. It seems 1992 was a good year for me when it came to matters of love: my diary records five separate events marked 'coronation day', complete with the initial and surname of the woman concerned. I remember only two women from that era – Busi and Hlengiwe. But I digress.

Here is what irked me about Busi that resulted in our needless altercation. We had made a plan to see each other one dull Friday evening. She was meant to spend the night at my place. At about 9:30 p.m., I arrived at our mutually agreed location, but there was no sign of Busi. I waited in vain. On my way back home, I made a decision that I would come to regret for the rest of my life. I decided that Busi's non-appearance was a serious transgression that required stern action. The misogynistic voice in my head believed, quite wrongly, that I had been kind enough, as I had given her four days to come up with a plausible excuse, and she hadn't.

The following Friday afternoon, I met up with Busi with the sole intention of raising the issue of her failure to honour our previous Friday-night appointment. The meeting place was our high school. I found her waiting for me behind the Standard 6 block, a spot that offered some privacy. By the time I approached her, I was already seething with anger, which had been building for the past six days. I bombarded her with a series of questions. There was really no time for her to answer the barrage of questions posed by this angry monster. In the heat of the moment, without any further thought, I raised not only my voice, but my hand. I punched and slapped her face repeatedly, and kicked her. She cried. I found it hard to stop, but when she started bleeding, sanity dawned. At that moment, I was immediately ashamed and full of remorse.

Despite this feeling of remorse, the 'big boys' tradition' decreed that I had to depart the crime scene at once, leaving no trace of my existence or actions. According to what was a widely accepted tradition, a girl, after having had an altercation with or being beaten by her boyfriend, was not allowed to report the incident to her teachers or parents. If, for whatever reason, a girl dared to report such an incident and the boy got into trouble, more trouble would befall the girl.

After the Busi episode, I made a vow that I have kept to this day: never to raise a hand to a woman. After the assault, our 'love affair' continued to stumble along as though nothing had happened. I never apologised for my actions. She never asked for an apology. I did not expect her to.

This is my only chance to say that I am sorry.

Our affair came to a screeching halt in early 1993, because of widespread claims that she was pregnant. The rumours spread like wildfire. I asked her about it, but she flatly denied it. Our relationship became strained and then died what I thought was a natural death. She never delivered any baby. Nonetheless, rumour-mongers accused her of having had an abortion. The truth is still unknown.

Fast-forward to 1996. We had rekindled our 'love affair'; Busi had not yet learnt to kiss. Truth be told, she remained my girlfriend for one reason and one reason only – she had money to throw around. She visited me every month-end and would leave behind a whopping R1 000.

Today, I confess I was once a blessee. My blesser was Busi. Don't laugh. I was on a R1 000 monthly allowance. For my sins, I almost had my tongue amputated; she would wrestle with it until it bled. That was almost twenty-two years ago. The blesser–blessee phenomenon is as old as prostitution itself. Don't judge me.

Things took a nasty turn again later that year. Busi phoned me in a state; I invited her to come and see me. At the time, I was living at Technikon Natal's Corlo Court residence in Durban. She lived out of town. She came to see me the very next day. That night, she broke down and cried.

'What's wrong, babes?'

Between sobs, Busi blurted out the words that would change our relationship forever: 'Bheki, I am pregnant.'

I was stunned. Firstly, since we had rekindled our 'love affair', we had always used protection. I had become wary of girlfriends, so condom usage had become standard, what with always getting sexually transmitted diseases. I explained to Busi that I was very sceptical about accepting responsibility, as we both knew we had used protection. At some stage I fell asleep. At the crack of dawn, when I woke up, Busi was still crying. This time, her eyes were red. Realising the gravity of the situation, I said to Busi that, if the child was mine, 'Well, you know my family.' It is now history that Busi never reported that pregnancy to my family. In fact, in December of that year I learnt from my friends, who were Busi's neighbours, that she was seeing someone else and it was no secret. At the time of this saga, Busi was a teacher in Ulundi.

Sadly, her child died before the age of five.

In 2012, in a routine consultation with my faith healer, Sis Dora, she claimed that I had a child who had died and that no proper burial rituals had been performed for him. I probed Dora to give me a picture of the woman in question. Dora insisted that I knew exactly which woman she was referring to, hinting that the event dated back to 1992. In a process of elimination, I zeroed in on Busi. After making some enquiries with my old eHabeni friends, I got Busi's number. I phoned her at once. I insisted on seeing her, as there was something huge we had to discuss. She wouldn't budge. Later in the conversation, I learnt that she was getting married that very weekend.

Nonetheless, I told her what my faith healer had told me. She dismissed my faith healer's message as that of a daydreamer, and said that Sis Dora should go back to the school where she learnt the art of interceding with the ancestors. So, the mystery of whether Busi was pregnant in 1992 remains unsolved. The issue of my mysterious child who demands burial rituals has not been taken any further. It is one of those things that haunt me in my sleep.

On the eve of her marriage, Busi confided in me that she still had feelings for me. She recounted all the significant moments that had happened in my life since we had broken up, as though she had had me followed. I told her that she was mad. All I wanted to know was whether she had ever had an abortion in her life, and whether the foetus that had died a terrible death was mine. But I will never know the truth.

READERS' RESPONSES

Bheki Mbanjwa: R1 000 monthly allowance??? You were earning a salary mos. Mina 17 years ago I was doing my internship and I think I was earning R1 500 and I was happy with that amount.

Zaheera Walker: You amuse me.

Sihle Boyah Ndlovu: My Blesser was a teacher as well in 2003.

26

Lindiwe: The antics of a crazy ex-girlfriend

At the precise moment, on 4 May 1997, that I laid eyes on Lindiwe, I became convinced that, after her, there could not be another woman. As André Brink writes in his book *Before I Forget*, '[t]here was nothing melodramatic about the acknowledgement: it was very calm, unemotional, and precise'. I knew instinctively in that split second that she was *the one* – the love of my life. In my head, she retorted, 'I am dark, but lovely.'

Lindiwe adorned her neck with chains of gold. She smelled of expensive cologne. She oozed confidence. She spoke in a deliberate manner – pronouncing each word perfectly, as if speaking to a child with special educational needs. I longed to touch her – to caress her and kiss her lovely lips from sunset till sunrise.

Lindiwe was the epitome of what boys in my 'hood call a dark beauty. She was slender, tall and blessed with a beautiful set of extraordinary white teeth. She wore her hair long.

It took longer than expected for me to make my move on Lindiwe. Nonetheless, we became friends instantly. About eight months after our chance encounter at the house of MaMkhulu (my sister's mom) in the informal settlement of Ohlange (Inanda) north of Durban, we embraced, and kissed. It was spontaneous. It felt natural. Our eyes locked. Neither of us moved. Neither of us uttered a word. Then we kissed again; with each kiss, the time lapse between one kiss and the next narrowed. Intuitively, we both bemoaned the time we'd wasted. I felt that honey and milk were under Lindiwe's tongue. I felt new and rejuvenated. Love was in the air. The scent of her perfume seemed to be a part of the charm conspiracy to draw me closer to her. It was overwhelming and inviting.

I was in love.

At first, my love affair with Lindiwe was exciting. We became good friends. We shared stories of heartache inflicted upon us by previous lovers. We did everything together – going to town, doing the washing, running general errands. We seemed to enjoy each other's company. I introduced her to current affairs, which meant we could discuss some interesting political developments. We even started a book club. We devoured all the Mills & Boon novels in our local library. There was only one thing at the time that didn't work for Lindiwe: she couldn't cook. I ate the food she cooked once, and vowed never to do so again. I learnt later that her father, not her mother, did all the cooking if he was at home. Lindiwe also knew about my other sexual liaisons and didn't kick up a fuss. On the surface, it looked like a mature relationship that could withstand any storm. But there was something about it I couldn't quite put my finger on.

There was a time when I reasoned that, if I listened to the silences for long enough, they would reveal to me what it meant to love Lindiwe. She had come into my life when the chips were really down. I was a varsity dropout. I was unemployed, probably unemployable. I had long since separated from the love of my life, Miss M. I was lonely. I needed to be needed. I needed to be useful, even if temporarily. I was living on a staple diet of dagga, booze and sex. Indeed,

I was a broken man living in the broken community of Ohlange. I wondered aloud what I lacked as a human being. Had I entered a second existence, characterised by a longing to belong to a world I had never experienced? Was I even living, or just consuming oxygen? Was this my life – as an angry, embittered black man in post-apartheid South Africa? Lindiwe was – or, rather, became – the epitome of my brokenness. She had no desire to see us 'working out'. All she ever wanted was sex, sex and more sex. I obliged.

After twelve months of being with Lindiwe, I no longer recognised the person I had become. I had lost 10 kilograms. It started slowly. We would meet for the night in her shack on the days her father was not at home (Lindiwe's father was cheating on his wife). The arrangement worked well at first. It meant we could spend a night together at least twice a week.

However, Lindiwe's father began disappearing for five full days a week, so I was expected to deliver in the bedroom for five long days in a row. The grand idea – that we were making use of stolen moments fruitfully – became academic. I must admit, at first I was a willing participant. Later, I was nothing but a passenger on a journey to Neverland.

I realised that Lindiwe had a desire to be needed, and that I had to fill that void. For her, sex with me became a panacea for all the societal ills bedevilling Ohlange. The situation worsened, as we started making love everywhere we went – parks, soccer grounds, toilets, etc. Once, security guards caught us in the park, stark naked. They called the police, who threatened to arrest us for what they called public indecency. Up until this point, I hadn't known that Lindiwe was an accomplished actor. She cried – okay, scratch that, she wailed, wailed and wailed – until the police announced, 'Abort the mission.' We were allowed to go. Hardly five minutes later,

Lindiwe was so composed, it was as if nothing had happened. In the taxi back to Ohlange, she was all over me. Yes, kissing me in a taxi full of strangers.

Barely a week after our brush with the law, Lindiwe pulled another stunt. She sent her younger sister to my house to signal that we had to meet in our designated spot. Remember, Lindiwe and I were meant to be *secret* lovers. I must say, it was the worst-kept secret ever. I abandoned whatever I was doing to attend to this emergency. Upon my arrival, Lindiwe was in a mean mood. Okay, she was as angry as a spinster. When I enquired about the nature of my transgression, she stunned me.

'You don't trust me. I know it. Don't even deny it.'

'What do you mean, babes?'

'When you are with me, why do you use a condom? I am sick and tired of this. I want out.'

'Okay, babes. Let us talk about this. I trust you. No more condoms from tonight.'

Well, I got a nasty STI that night. Lindiwe had become the second woman to gift me with one. Clearly, she was seeing someone else. Please don't ask me how and when. I thought we were spending all the hours available in a day together. After I reported my STI to her, our relationship entered a thawing period. Despite this, we continued on and off. But during this cooling-off period, another drama unfolded.

Fast-forward to a lovely overcast afternoon. Yes, I was back at Lindiwe's shack. This time around, I had brought insurance of some sort – my cousin – just in case things went haywire. We exchanged pleasantries. Lindiwe smiled, and the scent of her perfume overwhelmed me, bringing back all the happy memories. She ushered us inside. I intuitively celebrated this minor achievement – I knew in that moment that Lindiwe wanted our 'arrangement' to continue, despite the fact that I was not alone. Well, the cover story I had given my cousin for the reason we were going to Lindiwe's place was to ask her to buy us some beers. I asked. She obliged.

We sat chatting the afternoon away with the cold beers, and then … knock, knock, knock. Eish! Lindiwe answered the door, and a man unfamiliar to me ushered himself in and sat down on the beer crate. Lindiwe's mood changed. She no longer wore a smile, but rage. Fire! The unfamiliar man said he had a message for Lindiwe and requested to deliver it in private. Lindiwe interjected and said go ahead and deliver the message right here, because these two are going nowhere. The message: 'Mandla wants to see you.'

At that moment, Lindiwe lost it and yelled, 'Angisamfuni. (Tell him I no longer love him. He must leave me alone.)' We sat there, quiet as landmines after the war. The poor guy was shocked; he politely stood up and left. We continued with our chit-chat and, of course, the cold beers.

Suddenly, there was a commotion outside. Lindiwe rushed to the door to investigate. We followed her. There he was, in person – yes, the boyfriend, Mandla. Within seconds, a screaming match between Lindiwe and Mandla had ensued. The neighbours watched the spectacle with amusement. We stood there, motionless. After what amounted to an hour-long shouting match, Mandla finally got the message. He left with his dignity in tatters. We went back to the shack and resumed our meaningless chat and beer-drinking, in that order, as if nothing had happened.

Then it hit me. Lindiwe was absolutely crazy. She had multiple personalities, all competing for existence simultaneously.

In hindsight, Lindiwe and I were not an item; we had nothing more than a sexual arrangement. While stocks lasted, it worked like a charm. Nonetheless, Lindiwe had ravished my heart. Despite the fact that she had never sung to me, her presence in my life invoked in me the Songs of Solomon: in my imagination, Lindiwe's love was 'better than wine'. The two months I had spent deprived of sexual intercourse with Lindiwe during the cooling-off period made my imagination go into overdrive. All I could hear when I listened to the silences was a melody with these muddled verses from the Songs of Solomon: 'I have come to my garden, my love. I have gathered my myrrh with my spice. I have eaten my honeycomb with my honey. I have drunk my wine with my milk.'

Despite what had become obviously narcissistic behaviour on Lindiwe's side, I longed for her love. Although my memory fails me in terms of what happened to our arrangement after Lindiwe and Mandla's shouting match, by 2000, I could no longer hold back. I hunted Lindiwe down for a meeting. But I noticed something had shifted – she gave me a weak hug, and no kiss. I had imagined that our reunion would reignite the fire between us. But within minutes it became clear that she was no longer a happy chappy. I still remember our meeting as if it happened yesterday. We met at the Technikon Natal cafeteria. By this time, I was in my second year of journalism studies. I had regained some semblance of a normal life. My confidence was up after I had been awarded a coveted international scholarship to complete my degree. Most importantly, I had a room of my own, so privacy was guaranteed.

During our interaction, Lindiwe was reserved and spoke only if spoken to. I was aware that she had a new live-in boyfriend. I was desperate for her love – so much so that I was prepared to park in the same lane as the other guy. We agreed that Lindiwe would go away and rethink our relationship, and get back to me. I must admit, I was hopeful that we would get back together.

Days and days passed, and there was no indication that she'd try talking to me again. My phone calls went unanswered. Days became months; I gave up hope that Lindiwe and I would ever be a couple again. She had broken my fragile heart – it yearned for her love, but there was zilch I could do about it. Dulling the pain was the fact that, in any event, I still had high hopes that I would keep my promise not to date anyone until I had completed my studies. So, I was conflicted, but the hormones had other ideas.

It took me by surprise, therefore, when Lindiwe decided to make a bid for my love again a year later, but without bothering to talk to me first. She was still involved with her live-in lover. The rumour mill was spreading the news that I had moved on and begun dating a white woman. True to her crazy nature, perhaps, she decided to make a bid for my heart in unorthodox ways.

I became aware of Lindiwe's intentions by accident, after a series of strange events. Unbeknown to me, in 2001 Lindiwe was back in my life – this time, for good. She had invaded my dreams. I was sick and tired of dreaming about sexual intercourse with her, with a variety of strangers, and even with the shadows of women. Yes, I confess, I had wet dreams for a very long time. These wet dreams were disturbing, to say the least. They affected my quality of life and dealt a huge blow to my confidence and general demeanour. My attempts at getting to the bottom of these dreams took me to many faith healers and traditional healers. I lost count of the cleansing ceremonies I undertook with different healers. The common feature of all these failed cleansing ceremonies was that I was asked to bury my underwear at the river where the cleansing took place. Yet the dreams carried on as though they were on steroids. Yes, you guessed it: Lindiwe had bewitched me. I only became aware of this fact when I went to consult Sis Dora. She had come highly recommended.

During my consultation with Sis Dora, a prototype of my enemy was created. The picture fitted Lindiwe. I had been bewitched by a sorceress, I was told. Immediately after my consultation, I had a conference call with Lindiwe, Sis Dora, my friend Ntokozo Gwala and my cousin. I confronted Lindiwe about the sorceress and threatened her with physical violence.

She confessed: 'Yes, Bheki, it is all true. I went to the sangoma [sorceress] in Africa [a village near Inanda]. She told me that her muti would make you love me for the rest of my life. We had done all the rituals to make you come back to me, except I hadn't achieved the ultimate aim of sleeping with you so that all the muti could be transferred to you. My sorceress is now dead. I am sorry.'

I am still baffled as to why Lindiwe resorted to a sorceress to win me back. As I have disclosed, a year earlier I had poured my heart out, pleading with her for us to get back together. By this time, she was a third-year varsity student at the University of Durban-Westville. Back in 1998, I had convinced her and her parents that there was no point in keeping Lindiwe at home with such good matric results. They agreed, on condition that I helped her to obtain government funding for her studies. This was easy peasy lemon squeezy for me. It took me one trip to the university; I introduced Lindiwe to my comrades. I told them that Lindiwe was my sister, and that she needed hand-holding to get government funding. The comrades were eager to help, so Lindiwe was sorted. I explained to her parents that they had to fund-raise for her transport to varsity and general upkeep. They kept their part of the bargain. But I digress.

I am still trying to figure out Lindiwe's motive for bewitching me without even attempting to rekindle the old flames of love in orthodox ways. Nonetheless, after her confession, I forgave her and moved on. Four years ago, I bumped into Lindiwe by chance. By this time, she had a new boyfriend and was working as a teacher. True to Lindiwe's crazy nature, she introduced me to her new boyfriend as her uncle. I wasn't surprised. Her behaviour confirmed that she really was nuts. I just gave up.

READERS' RESPONSES

Noloyiso Mtembu: I would buy this book. Beautiful ?? I can see Lindiwe in my head. You've placed me in the setting ?? Love is a beautiful thing, isn't it?

Kolisa Nokoyo: 'I abandoned whatever I was doing to attend to this emergency.' This got me into stitches. I can't wait for more. If there's a book I'm on the waiting list.

Sandile Zulu: What a fantastic read, very well written, can't wait for part 2 …

Sizwe Mncube Mzilankatha: I am looking forward to reading more of your well thought writings you share my brother. It's not only good stories but also a lecture on the art of writing.

Jabulile Maluleka: Hahahaha! Wow! What a riveting love story. If it was a book I wouldn't have been able to put it down. You're a gifted storyteller.

Rethabile Matolweni: Beautiful piece of writing sir.

Nombuso MaMshengu Shabalala: Captivating writing!! I love it.

Amelia Naidoo: I'm rushing to get ready to meet a friend for dinner BUT I had to stop to read this to the very end. Great writing. Looking forward to part two.

Busani Ngcaweni: Is it possible that Lindiwe was overwhelmed by your obsessive love? Remember she didn't have a father so she had no reference point of affection from a male figure? Lindiwe, oh Lindiwe! You beautiful lady of contradictions!

27

Lerato: A fleeting love affair

Women have been in and out of my bedroom, literally and figuratively, but not one has had the same impact as Lerato, in the shortest possible time. My fleeting love affair with Lerato began and ended at the honeymoon stage. All in all, it lasted no more than four hours. Yes, you read that one right: I once had a sexual relationship with a woman that lasted the whole of four hours. This was almost twenty years ago, yet I remember it as if it happened yesterday. Don't call me wacky just yet. Instead, get some popcorn, sit back and let me tell you my story.

I refuse to call my sexual relationship with Lerato a one-night stand. It wasn't. In fact, there was no night involved at all. Ours was nothing more than an intensely carnal encounter.

One ordinary day, on the mean streets of Ohlange, north of Durban, I took my daily morning walk to the local spaza shop to buy bread. I was wearing a revealing pair of Moroka Swallows shorts and no top. I had the confidence of a cat, because I was training in those days. Let's just say I had something to show – maybe not a six-pack, but something close. I hadn't even taken a shower. This was also routine. The shop was literally metres away from my humble abode. I had no idea that I would meet any woman remotely interested in a relationship with me, let alone one who was prepared to open her bedroom for me. So, I wasn't looking. The last thing on my mind was meeting a woman and negotiating an affair. At worst, I expected a chance encounter with many a sexual partner in the neighbourhood who wouldn't kick up a fuss about me walking the streets before taking a shower. My morning walk to the spaza was meant to be as routine as possible. It turned out to be anything but.

As I crossed what masqueraded as a main road, despite it being nothing more than one lane, half-tarred and half-gravel, I locked eyes with a passer-by. Intuitively, I stopped dead in my tracks. The passer-by was a woman, possibly in her twenties. I had no doubt that she was new to the neighbourhood. She stopped, too – for entirely different reasons, perhaps. I didn't give her the third-degree to find out why she'd stopped. The whole thing seemed like some choreo-graphed scene straight out of a Hollywood movie. For a minute, neither of us uttered a word.

But something had to give. So, I decided to man up and break the ice with a customary 'Hello, beautiful!' She smiled and asked if I was a charmer boy. I smiled back, and said it depends. As we spoke, I studied her intently. She was a fine woman with a sexy body to die for. She was also tall, light-skinned, curvy, with curly hair. When she smiled, cute dimples formed on her cheeks. When she wasn't smiling, you were confronted with a dignified presence; she oozed confidence and class. Although she wore simple jeans and a nondescript top, she made the top look good on her. She was picture perfect – a strong, independent, yet funny woman. I was captivated by her. For a second, I forgot about my near-nakedness and the fact that I hadn't even brushed my teeth, let alone taken a shower.

I stood there, motionless and at a loss for words. She said, 'Ye, *boet*, if you have anything to say to me, please go ahead, because I am in a hurry.'

I could immediately detect by her accent that she was not Zulu. She sounded Xhosa, but in fact she was Sotho, and spoke isiZulu, isiXhosa and a combination of Setswana and Sepedi fluently. I mumbled something about her being new to the neighbourhood. She confirmed at once that she was visiting an aunt. Apparently, her aunt lived a mere kilometre from where we were standing. I was so overwhelmed by her stage presence that I started by apologising.

'I am sorry to be forward, but I would really love to meet and talk to you. Don't get me wrong – this is not what I routinely do to all beautiful women.'

Of course, I was lying through my teeth. By late 1997, I was a fully fledged Casanova.

Out of the blue, she smiled and said, 'I believe you.'

As soon as she uttered those words, I saw a gap and, like a true professional philanderer, I pounced on her. I told her that she was the most beautiful woman I had ever laid eyes on. I described each feature of hers that I loved. She was blown away, giggling, smiling and laughing all the way through my pitch. Unbeknown to her, my pitch was nothing new – it was standard operating procedure. It went something like this: if you meet a new woman, tell her she is more beautiful than all your former girlfriends combined. As soon as you've said this, you must pause; if she laughs, you're onto something. Then pull out card number two: find something about her that stands out for you.

For Lerato, I told her she made those jeans and top look good. She was beautiful inside out, I added nonchalantly. I promised her that, if she were to become my girlfriend, I would stop my philandering at once. By this stage, she was laughing uncontrollably.

She retorted: 'Look, because you made me laugh, I will give you a chance. Here is my number. Don't call me tonight. In fact, come and see me at seven o'clock tomorrow morning. Before I change my mind, please walk me to my aunt's place.'

I obliged. My loins were on fire for the whole fifteen minutes of our walk. At some stage, she noticed that my member was up and, without mincing her words, said: 'We will see tomorrow morning if you can perform; you seem too eager.'

At that point, I knew I had scored the ultimate yet most unexpected prize. The reaction of my body meant that we were, indeed, sexually compatible.

The whole scene blew me away. I couldn't believe that my routine morning walk had taken such an unexpected turn. I could see a friendly fire in her eyes. As I smelled her cologne, its scent invited me to navigate the contours of her anatomy. I immediately started counting the hours. The countdown to seven o'clock started at exactly nine thirty-two that morning.

An hour had passed since I'd left home to buy bread. By the time I arrived back at the house, there was consternation on the part of MaMkhulu. I told her some white lies about my whereabouts to account for the whole hour I had been away. I said something about an old friend I had bumped into, and that we'd had a lot of catching up to do. My mom accepted my explanation. She was only too happy that I hadn't been harmed.

I was in a state of ecstasy the whole day. I made breakfast, cleaned the house and made dinner. I did my routine walk to the library with Lindiwe to return books and borrow some more. Throughout all these activities, I was counting down to seven o'clock the next morning. I told nobody about my chance encounter with Lerato and the possibility of the next morning's bountiful harvest.

At five o'clock the next day, I was up. I trained with my cousin for an hour. After training, I took a shower. At exactly six forty-five, I quietly left the house. The moment of truth had arrived. I was the man of the hour. Fifteen minutes later, I knocked on the shack that Lerato had told me was her temporary abode when she visited her aunt. The voice on the inside said come in, the door is open.

I hesitated for a moment. Then, I pushed the door open and walked in. Whoa, Lord! Lo and behold, she was taking a bath, completely naked. My presence did not affect her at all. She remained calm and jovial. She even apologised for not having made the bed. But I wasn't listening. My mind was fixed on the ultimate prize. This, dear reader, is the kind of thrill that keeps philanderers in business.

As soon as she was done bathing, without a care in the world she walked around the place, tying up some loose ends. Suddenly, she said, 'Stand up and give a girl a hug.' I obliged. For the next three hours, I navigated the contours of her anatomy. We went the whole way, as though we had rehearsed our moves. Such sexual compatibility is hard to come by. I was over the moon.

By the time Ukhozi FM said it was ten o'clock, Lerato pulled away, gave me a lazy smile, and whispered sweet nothings into my left ear. It was time to call it quits. During the marathon three hours, she had called the shots. She was in charge. She knew what she wanted, and how. Clearly, she was no amateur in the business of intensely carnal affairs. I was more than satisfied. In fact, I felt like I was on top of the world. Look what you have done, Johnny, clever boy! The T-shirt I had been wearing during the marathon session had become soaked in sweat at some point. My worry was now how to explain it to strangers. For my family, I had a cover story to say I had decided to take a morning run. But I digress.

At exactly 10:05 a.m., I waved goodbye to Lerato. She planted a kiss on my forehead and mumbled something like 'thank you'. I reciprocated by telling her that she was simply the best, and that there would be nobody after her. We both laughed at our own lies.

I left. And so did Lerato. She left town that same day, without saying goodbye. Afterwards, I tried her cellphone several times, but it went straight to voicemail. I canvassed the neighbourhood door to door to ascertain whether anyone had a forwarding address or an alternative number. It seemed that nobody knew anything about Lerato, including her supposed aunt. All my detective work came to nought. I have not seen Lerato nor heard from her since that eventful day. She simply disappeared off the face of the earth.

But she left a lasting impression. She gave me four hours to treasure for all my philandering years, making her anything but a fleeting love affair.

28

The anatomy of lust: Sex and money

As I got closer to her, my senses were overwhelmed by the smell of cigarettes, sweat and booze. I must admit that I was little bit shy and slightly nervous. At that stage, I could have retreated and looked for another girl. But although I was fearful and naive, there was no turning back. In any event, I was completely single-minded: I was going to get laid that night, by hook or by crook. In fact, I was resolute that I was going to pay for sex that night. Finish and *klaar*!

I didn't notice anything remotely attractive about her, but then the transaction was being conducted in the dark. All I could make out was that she was nothing like those ladies I had seen in porn movies. This bothered me. I wondered to myself why anyone would pay money to have sex with her. Deep down in my heart, I knew she wasn't the best choice. However, my choices were limited, because I didn't know any better. This was my first time scouting the streets of Durban at night, specifically looking for a sex worker.

I had fear in my heart. I feared getting arrested for solicitation of prostitution. I feared the pimps. I feared the drug lords who apparently roam the streets at night. I feared the sex workers' community. Above all, I feared being noticed by someone who knew me. Basically, I was in panic mode; nonetheless, I was determined to do the deed.

I had this insatiable desire to pay for sex that night. To this day, I have no idea what had got into me.

At the time, I had a semblance of a normal life. I had left the dungeon of Ohlange, north of Durban, where my life had been characterised by booze, dagga and easy women. I guess old habits die hard. In my new life, I had committed myself to sexual abstinence – or so I thought. The project had gone smoothly for some months. I had no girlfriend and I wasn't looking. I was the epitome of a single, satisfied and independent (SSI) man.

Yes, I confess, I paid a woman so that I could have sex with her. I am therefore complicit in the act of prostitution. Today, I can comprehend why women enter prostitution, as modern research concludes that they do so for various reasons, the most common being unemployment or a desire to improve their income. It is also believed that some women are victims of human trafficking. It is therefore irresponsible to judge these women while their male clients get off scot-free, remaining anonymous.

Dear reader, the fact of the matter is that I paid a woman to have sex with me, and this is the truth, the whole truth and nothing but the truth. It was my decision and my decision alone. No peer pressure. Zilch. Nada. It was a military-style operation, as no one knew about my whereabouts that night. I left the comfort of my home and walked the streets of Durban looking for the ladies of the night. I wasn't even sure which streets were frequented by these ladies. Nonetheless, I was hell-bent on finding out for myself what was so special about a woman who sells sex for a living. I walked the streets armed only with a condom and sexual cravings. I was feeling the torment of my own raging lust.

To say the experience was underwhelming is to put it mildly. After I had paid the compulsory R50 fee upfront, I was hauled into a passage and told to make it quick. She didn't even look me in the eye. I had expected some form of foreplay to prepare both of us. So I was shocked when she removed her underwear and slowly bent over. I had imagined that we would go to some secluded, cheap accommodation for the act. I was wrong. Nonetheless, I had had experience of sexual encounters in open spaces – twice before. The only difference was that these two sexual encounters were by mutual agreement, and not a business transaction.

I realised early on that she had noticed my naivety and was just going to make a quick buck, then disappear into the darkness of the night. Fear set in, this time of my chosen lady of the night. A million thoughts raced through my mind. What if she stabbed me to death during the sexual encounter? What if she pulled a gun and robbed me? What if, what if, etc. So, I obeyed the command to get ready for a quickie. It was all over in less than five minutes. In hindsight, she, too, may have had her own fears, perhaps similar to mine.

Although I felt cheated, I was more than relieved that it was all over. Yes, I had paid R50 for an absolutely horror-filled experience. I had paid to have sexual pleasure and received none. But all I wanted after the deed was done, was to run for my life. I pulled up my pants and walked back into the light in the adjoining street. About 500 metres away from the scene of the crime, I started to run, although no one was chasing me. I ran all the way back to my residence. I felt dirty. I was in dire need of a shower, thinking that fresh water could somehow wipe the whole experience off my mind and body. My conscience sprang into action and said that what I had done was wrong. I still felt disgusted with myself after the shower.

However, I am not alone – either in having paid for sex or in feeling underwhelmed by the experience.

A major international research project, published in 2005, sought to uncover the reality of men who buy sex. The research project spanned six countries, targeting men between the ages of eighteen and seventy. It included men of all races – white, black, Asian and Eastern European; most were employed and many were educated beyond school level. In the main, they were presentable and polite, with average-to-good social skills. Many were husbands and boyfriends; just over half were either married or in a relationship with a woman. The research found that the number of men who pay for sex had doubled in a decade. The authors attributed this rise to 'a greater acceptability of commercial sexual contact', yet many of the interviewees concurred with me: they felt 'an intense guilt and shame about paying for sex'. Most of the men in the research universe found the experience of paying for sex 'unfulfilling, empty, and terrible'. This research report was published in *The Guardian* in 2010.

Years later, when I became a columnist, I made an impassioned public plea for the authorities to decriminalise sex work. Nonetheless, to this day, when I drive the streets at night and see sex workers on the side of the road, my senses are overwhelmed by the smell of smoke, sweat and booze. I regret my experiment, which was clearly driven by raging lust and nothing else.

29

A stranger in my bed: Love, lust and obsession

I had gone to sleep by myself, but when I was woken up at midnight, there was a stranger in my bed. Yes, a woman with whom I had no prior arrangements to share a bed had got into it, without me having noticed. Confounding the situation was that I shared a flat with a male friend, who had gone out for the night. He was as shocked as I was at the sight of the woman in our shared bedroom. We had a gentleman's agreement not to have any overnight female visitors in our flat.

After a cursory investigation, it became clear that I knew the woman. A month earlier, she had been a one-night stand. I had erroneously believed that we had both understood the limited prospects of casual hanky-panky. I had no reason to believe otherwise. In any event, she had told me in no uncertain terms that she was involved with someone else. Our dalliance was meant to be short-lived and sexual only.

At the time we had become physically involved, we were both vulnerable, in a way. We were far away from our familiar surroundings, involved in community development work at a student winter camp. I had known her informally for many months. I had not for one minute been physically, or otherwise, attracted to her.

At any rate, she was not my type of girl. It is beside the point that, at the time, I had made a vow not to get emotionally or sexually attached to any woman, as I wanted to focus all my energies on my studies. I was also low on confidence, due to the fact that I was flat broke. My vow of sexual abstinence had held for six months, until that fateful afternoon when my testosterone levels shot through the roof at the distant possibility that this woman was sexually attracted to me. In the heat of the moment, I decided to make an exception in her case.

Without discussing anything, we both instigated a plan to have time alone. So, when the other students went to the nearest shopping centre, we both stayed behind. I was eager to navigate the unknown with a woman I had barely considered as a sexual partner, let alone a lover. However, there seemed to be an eagerness driven by the newness of discovery, which I felt was mutual. I thanked my lucky stars that she had recognised the loneliness in me and was prepared to go the extra mile to make it vanish. All things being equal, I relented, and broke my vow. There wasn't even any pretence that we loved one another. We were both simply burning with physical lust.

I had no idea that she had an obsessive personality. For me, it was nothing more than a once-off, casual sexual arrangement. After our return from the winter camp, there was – in my mind, at least – no expectation that anything remotely relationship-like would happen.

However, there was strong mutual lust. I relented again, and slept with her after our one-night-stand agreement. I guess this was a turning point in our relationship: I ostensibly led her on to a point where she believed there was an 'us'. In her everyday behaviour, there was no hint that she was hypersexual or obsessed with me.

I should have known better. Our casual relationship had started in the bedroom; clearly, as an obsessive woman, she developed an emotional bond. Because of our physical intensity, she assumed that I was deeply in love with her. Psychologists have long concluded that obsessive lovers often rush into a sexual relationship before developing an emotional bond with their partners. These types of casual lovers mistake physical sexual encounters for love. Trying to connect the dots of her behaviour after the student camp, I should have seen the signs. (I didn't.) She managed to be in the vicinity of wherever I was. I spent a hell of a lot of time at the students' club offices, and she was always there. These accidental meetings didn't break her habit of checking up on me daily via cellphone to touch base and catch up, as it were.

But I am getting ahead of myself. Let me tell you how it all went down. On one dull Friday, I had decided to call it an early night. I slept on a mattress on the floor in my friend's flat; we shared the space. I must have gone to sleep at about 9 p.m. At some point during the night, it felt as though something or someone was touching me rather inappropriately. I just assumed that it was my flatmate, who perhaps was too drunk to hop onto the bed. In my sleepy state, I moved from the mattress and squeezed myself into the bed, which had a bunch of books piled on it. I didn't even move them; I squashed myself in, and continued sleeping.

At midnight, I was woken up by a commotion. As I awoke, I was shocked to see my flatmate standing at the door, looking dumbfounded. I took a look around. Lo and behold, there was a stranger tucked away on the mattress. I removed the sheet from its head, and made an astonishing find. There she was, sleeping peacefully, as though she owned the place. I woke her up and demanded that she leave at once. She didn't look particularly perturbed. I walked her halfway to her place. During our walk of shame, I probed her to find out what had happened. She said she couldn't sleep without me, so she had decided to come over. She admitted that, upon her arrival, I was fast asleep.

'I saw that you were sleeping peacefully, so I didn't want to disturb you. I simply joined you and felt safe,' she said.

It hit me that I was dealing with an obsessive woman. My anger dissipated immediately, and I laughed harder than I should have.

I explained to her that the golden cup hadn't broken – it hadn't existed in the first place. She understood the enormity of what she had done and mumbled an apology. We parted ways for good. She went on to find happiness elsewhere, and I moved on too.

30

Date my family: Love, lust and jealousy

You have seen that I was a Casanova in my heyday. However, even by my standards, getting caught up in a love triangle involving siblings was more than I'd ever bargained for. Wait for it: I met and fell in 'love' with two separate women on the same night in 1998. It was more like speed-dating, because it all materialised within one hour.

After the fact, I patted myself on the back for the bountiful harvest. I was salivating at the prospect of the upcoming dates with my brand-new 'girlfriends'. This all happened one night on the mean streets of Ohlange. I was in the good company of my cousin, a smooth talker of note.

In the still of the night, in spite of the street lights that functioned intermittently, Ohlange seemed to be an unfamiliar neighbourhood, especially if you were walking through it alone. This despite the fact that, in every third house – or, more appropriately, *mjondolo* (shack) – there was a tavern, bottle store or spaza shop. These were frequented by a variety of customers – lonely hearts, prostitutes, outlaws and outright dangerous characters. The sodium gleam of the street lights or the flickering strip light from a lone, passing VW Golf blasting music at over 105 decibels offered little consolation. As Matthew Beaumont wrote in *The Guardian*, describing the streets of London after dark, 'there were alleys and street corners and shop entrances where the darkness appears to collect in a solid mass'. Or, to take a haunting line from 'Alastor: Or, the Spirit of Solitude' by Percy Bysshe Shelley, 'night makes a weird sound of its own stillness'.

In the stillness of night, the streets of Ohlange smelled of danger, dagga, alcohol, and the blood of its own children.

It was in these streets where we hunted for lone walkers and easy women. Our nefarious plan for walking the streets at night was to collect cellphone numbers and propose a drink or two to the girls. We always banked on the hope that we would have our way with them later. More often than not, our strategy worked like a charm.

But nothing had prepared us for the eventuality that, one day, we would date a family. I couldn't believe it myself. For most philanderers, it's the thrill of a lifetime to date siblings. However, although I was a broken man living in a broken community, no number of sexual escapades with the siblings could wash away the guilt of the act itself. Yet I enjoyed the ecstasy while it lasted.

When this love triangle began, I was living on the edge of society, a life characterised by booze, dagga, easy money and easy women. Despite this, the community of Ohlange had respect for me and my cousin. I guess we were the better devils. We were infamous philanderers, but the community still considered us to be model youth – not members of any gang, not involved in crime, well dressed and articulate. We milked this perception for all it was worth. It made it easier for us to offer our free services to the lone walkers at night.

On one such walk, we bumped into a woman. She was extremely light in complexion, slender and quite tall. She was walking alone – easy prey.

We shouted, 'Hey, beautiful, it's dark. Can we walk with you?'

She agreed at once. We accompanied her for about two kilometres to her place. As per our routine, I got her cellphone number, and we agreed to meet again to explore a romantic relationship. My cousin and I then trekked back to our hunting ground.

Wow! Suddenly there was manna from heaven. We spotted three women walking alone in the opposite direction. We changed tack and offered to accompany the group to their destination. Unbeknown to us, this group of three women were all family, and among them was the mother of the girl we had just accompanied home. In this group, we managed to get the two younger girls' cellphone numbers.

During the walk, we became aware that the older woman was their mother. Luckily, she was a modern woman, so the girls were free to flirt with us and exchange phone numbers. At some point during our walk, they said that their home was in the same vicinity as the one in which we had left the first woman. Nothing clicked; they thanked us and we parted ways. We had already agreed to meet the younger girls for drinks the next day.

Later that evening, I received a call from the first girl – let's call her Malindi. She told me that her younger sister also had my number, and wanted to know how that had happened. At first, I was in the dark, until she explained that the group of three women we had accompanied home were her family. I had to spill the beans, but I assured her that my heart was with her, and not her younger sister. We ended the call on good terms.

The next day, I phoned the younger sister and explained that my heart was with her, not her older sister. She accepted my explanation. The love triangle was in full swing. I was beside myself with joy.

To complicate matters further, my cousin started dating the other sister, Xoli. So we were dating three women from one family at once.

Xoli was very smart and said nothing about my relationship with her sisters. She was only too happy to spend time with us, regardless of which sister was present.

For three months thereafter, I had to be very clever and set up an appointment with one of them only if I knew the other one was not available or was going to be somewhere else. But Malindi was no fool. She soon discovered that I was sleeping with her sister. During one of our late-afternoon rendezvous, she confronted me. I tried in vain to explain that it was 'complicated'. She said, 'I will make it easy for you.' She then handed me her cellphone and instructed me to tell her sister that, from now on, I was hers alone. I had no choice but to speak to her sister and explain that we were breaking up because I had chosen Malindi.

The very next day, I phoned the younger sister to explain myself. She said, 'Don't worry; I know you didn't mean what you said yesterday. It all came from my jealous sister.'

Our love triangle continued until it died a natural death, like all casual and intensely physical relationships.

31

Thandiwe: Like mother, like daughter

Thandiwe was a pretty young woman and a true yellow-bone, complete with blue eyes and a perfect set of white teeth. She was my dove, my perfect one. In her beauty, she looked like a delicate piece of art. I imagined she wasn't meant for hard labour, such as cooking or carrying wood or balancing buckets of water on her head. Yet I had seen her working hard, because we lived in an informal settlement where essential services were non-existent.

Thandiwe's natural beauty was complemented by her facial mole and the way she carried herself. Her eyes and cheekbones added an aura of sexiness. It didn't help that she had an eye for fashion, and wore her hair long in different styles. Although she was unemployed, she appeared, in her dress sense, to be a fashionista. To me, Thandiwe was there to be admired for her delicate, light complexion and what appeared, in my mind, to be an extraordinary beauty. Her skin looked too soft and precious. She seemed fragile. I loved her easy manner. She also didn't demand much of a man either emotionally or financially, making her a perfect candidate for the multiple-relationship landscape.

At the time, I wasn't aware of the public frenzy around dark-skinned versus light-skinned women. I was happy to have Thandiwe parked in the same lane as Lindiwe, the dark-skinned beauty queen.

Sadly, Thandiwe was a high-school dropout. She had fallen pregnant and borne a child at sixteen. She was now a single parent and a discouraged job-seeker. We struggled to converse for more than an hour at a time. Her life seemed to revolve around celebrities, women's magazines and, of course, the American soapie, *The Bold and the Beautiful*. Predictably, these were not issues in which I was well versed. I have always been a writer, so words about meaningful subjects of life, such as climate change and the possibility of World War III, have always been uppermost in my mind.

Throughout our love affair, we never discovered any common interests. We somehow enjoyed our singularity within a union. Although I was down and out, I kept up to date with politics and current affairs. I craved to crack a political joke or two. Just not with Thandiwe.

To make matters worse, she was terrible in bed. I guess, as André Brink writes in *Before I Forget*, 'sometimes to sleep with someone can be more intimate than making love'. So, she stayed put. But there was another, more sinister, reason for keeping her: to show her off to my friends just to prove that I could date any pretty young thing – yellow-bone, on top of that. Having multiple girlfriends was, at the time, a sure sign that you were alive and happening. Don't invoke the ethical question of multiple partners. Thandiwe was my girl-friend in my time of madness on the edge of society. Nobody gave a toss about my lifestyle, least of all Thandiwe. I opine that she, too, was seeing someone on the side. She even knew about Lindiwe. All she cared about was having her turn at the table unencumbered by the existence of the other women in my life. I managed to keep a tenuous peace between the light-skinned girlfriend and the dark beauty. Life was good.

However, my relationship with Thandiwe was lopsided. She was just there for my inner entertainment. It wasn't a reciprocal relationship at all. She lacked something that I couldn't put my finger on.

Which was true until she passed away unexpectedly. I was sad to lose her. But nothing in our relationship could have prepared me for what happened next. One night, on the streets of Inanda, many years after Thandiwe had passed on, I met a petite young yellow-bone. My heart mellowed at the mere sight of her. She looked about eighteen years old. I am not sure; the street lights in Inanda work intermittently. But I was truly captivated.

Without wasting time, I made my bid. I told her how I felt about her, and she giggled wryly. Moments after she had been swallowed by the darkness, my cousin told me who she was.

It was Thandiwe's daughter. She had grown up to be like her mother. As they say, the apple doesn't fall far from the tree. I may not have been known for my high moral standing at the time, but I still had an ounce of honour left. I deleted the young woman's cellphone number and made a vow that I wouldn't date her.

This piece is dedicated to the loving memory of Thandiwe. May her gentle soul rest in eternal peace.

32

Sebe: A player gets played

Sebenzile (Sebe) Gwala was my accidental girlfriend. I have no recollection of pursuing her. Instead, she made the first move, and chased
after me until the end.

I vividly remember the finer details of our chance encounter.
It was another ordinary Friday afternoon. Two fine-looking girls
stopped me dead in my tracks near Berea Centre in Durban. One
introduced herself as Sebe. She mumbled something about my elder
brother having dated a girl from her village back in Eshowe. She
sort-of intimated that she would love to talk to me sometime in
private. I couldn't have cared less, and let the moment pass.

In reality, I was completely consumed by my own thoughts. At
that very time, I had a rare chance to be by myself and was quietly
enjoying the serenity of it all. Honestly, I was too busy for a twenty-
something rural boy in the big city. I was serving on the executive
committees of Technikon Natal's SRC, SASCO, SASPU, the South
African Technikon Students' Union (SATSU) and the ANC, to name
just a few. Solitude to me was what thinners is to paint. As a result
of my political engagements, I was famous for always carrying two
diaries and chain-smoking. I was always on my way to a meeting,
on or off campus. There was a time in 1996, according to the finance

department, when I travelled outside of Durban more than Technikon Natal's principal, Professor Bennie Khoapa. But I digress.

As soon as Sebe left, it was a case of out of sight, out of mind. But it wasn't long before she made a second cameo appearance. This time, I wasn't alone. I was sitting in the cafeteria with my comrades when a tall, strikingly attractive, blue-eyed yellow-bone approached our table, arms wide open, ready for a hug. I was lucky that my memory saved me from embarrassment: I remembered her from our encounter a week earlier. I must admit, my heart skipped a beat. I was captivated by the sheer presence of this woman. She oozed class and sophistication. Something about her set her apart from the rest of the flock. I stood up and hugged her in return. She promised to come and see me in my office so that we could talk – don't ask me about what, exactly. I was too starstruck to say anything. I later learnt that she was a professional model.

Two things struck me about Sebe. She was bold and uncompromising in pursuing a love affair with me. And she was a typical model-like beauty – slender and tall, with long legs and a flat stomach. Exactly what the love doctor ordered. There was more to Sebe, though, than just a pretty face. She may have been beautiful on the outside, but her beauty reached all the way into the depths of her soul. As they say, true beauty comes from within. She radiated a certain grace, a contained passion and sexuality. I liked her, but I had a lot on my plate. Those were fair times for me. I dated any woman I fancied. I had power, money and the charm of a budding politician.

I really have no memory of what tilted the scales in Sebe's favour. But there was one atypical thing about her that perturbed me in all the years I dated or knew her: whenever I was around her, I was a nervous wreck. Yes, you read that right. Every time I was about to meet her, I would start having heart palpitations. At first, it was intriguing. Later, I put it down to pure witchcraft.

Lo and behold! Sebe arrived in my SRC presidential office one day, unannounced. I was doing routine students' consultations. There was always a queue of students waiting for me during the predetermined consultation times. I had no warning of who was coming in or the issues they would bring. In my usual boisterous voice, I shouted 'Next!', and boom, boom, boom! Sebe appeared out of the blue. She walked in as though she owned the place. She was in high heels and dressed to the nines. I had never seen such confidence in any woman before. She immediately closed the door behind her and took a seat. She looked me straight in the eye and said, 'I thought I should come and say hi.'

She spoke and I listened. The temperature – or, rather, the heat – shot through the roof, despite the fact that the air conditioner was always set at nineteen degrees. I was sweating and trembling. Something had to give: I summoned enough courage and uttered the following words: 'Perhaps you can join me for a movie tomorrow.'

She rolled her big eyes as though she was paging through an imaginary electronic diary, and calmly said, 'Are you asking me on a date, Mr Mncube?'

I was speechless. She looked bullish; I was on the back foot yet again. I retorted, 'Consider it my treat for being my homegirl. It would be nice to spend time together and to get to know each other better.'

She said yes as if it was no big deal. We exchanged telephone numbers and parted ways.

I remember nothing about the movie I watched with Sebe. My heart was racing. All I really wanted to do was to cuddle up to her and kiss her soft, lovely lips. After the movie, like true students, we stopped at Musgrave Centre and grabbed some pizza, then walked together to our respective residences.

Soon, my focus shifted to the next big moment. How on earth were we going to part ways? Was it going to be a kiss on the cheek, or the real thing? The big moment arrived. There I was, standing at her door, behaving like a pre-teen falling in love for the first time. I think she sensed that I was nervous. She opened her arms wide; I moved in like a forklift. I hugged her for what appeared to be minutes on end. As I pulled away, at the speed of light, she gave me a full-mouth kiss. It felt extraordinarily special. I knew deep down in my heart that she had just joined my exclusive club of girlfriends. I went back to my residence with my confidence sky-high. I should have known better.

Nothing could have prepared me for Sebe's next thunderbolt. It was a script straight out of the movies. Until that moment, I had managed my love affairs quietly and without much fanfare. Sebe told me that there was a modelling event at the Sports Centre on the weekend, and asked me to accompany her. I agreed at once. I shouldn't have. We made all the arrangements and met just outside the Sports Centre. She draped her figure around mine and we entered the packed Sports Centre like a Hollywood couple. There was whistling and ululating. I had to walk her all the way to the stage, and then I was ushered into the front-row seats reserved for VIPs. Clearly, this carefully choreographed late entrance was meant for her to mark her territory. Suddenly, all and sundry knew that we were dating. I had no clue that Sebe was the kind of girl who loved wearing her heart on her sleeve.

Well, Sebe wasn't done with her trickery. For some odd reason, I decided to leave the event early after she had assured me that she had made proper security arrangements to get back to her flat.

At exactly 1:39 a.m., I heard a knock on my door. In a petulant mood, I woke up and opened the door. As I opened it, her light complexion lit up the darkness. She had decided that going to her place wasn't a good idea; she would rather spend the night with me. I asked no questions. She walked in and kissed me on my cheek as if to say, 'Big boy, don't you worry. You will be fine.' I didn't know the protocol – whether to take off my pyjamas and jump into bed, or switch off the lights to allow her to change. All I was thinking was that clearly the heavens had opened for me. I felt like the luckiest man alive. In the end, we snuggled up in bed like true lovers, but I never had access to the velvet cake.

At the crack of dawn, she announced that she was leaving. Apparently, her father's brother – some run-of-the-mill politician – had a tendency to check up on her in the mornings before he went to work. I accompanied Sebe to her place. During our short walk of shame (on my part), I kept asking myself a million questions about her early-morning behaviour. I am still baffled about why she came all the way to my place in the wee hours of the morning if not to let go of the main prize.

After these events, the talk on campus was all about Stalin's new model girlfriend. I was thrust into the limelight for dating a model, something completely new to me. I had been known for my political work, not for frivolities. Sebe never let up on showing me off. I now had a new schedule: attending modelling events, including auditions. The talk on campus was now all about the famous hand-holding couple. I hated it. Simultaneously, I liked it. It felt almost as if it gave me an aura of respectability. I have always been a closet celebrity.

In the end, Sebe became an emotional burden. I was a young, hot-blooded philanderer, yet she refused to have sex with me, even after the infamous ninety-day rule had lapsed. This rule states that women should wait ninety days before giving away the 'cookie'. In spite of this, our love affair remained the stuff of gossip-mongers. In hindsight, our relationship was a public-relations exercise for Sebe – nothing more, nothing less: 'See, I am dating the SRC president and there is nothing you can do about it.'

Furthermore, when Sebe left me, it was also an agonisingly protracted process. Years after all the drama on campus, our on-and-off love affair continued lurching from one near disaster to the next.

It was maybe three years after our campus days when we hooked up again. She was now a young working adult. I was at her flat in Ulundi, where she gave me every indication that, finally, we were going to go all the way. She whispered in my ear that I must come to her flat first thing in the morning, before 6 a.m. I understood, because there were other people in her flat at the time. I was over the moon. I arrived at her place the next morning at 5:31 a.m. I knocked once, and she immediately answered the door. And, and oh, my God, the girl was in her birthday suit. I was mesmerised. I told myself that, finally, it was all going to go down.

But I was wrong. I joined her in her bed, but nothing happened. Zilch, zip, nada! She told me a very long, complex story about the absence of sex in our relationship, and how it was making it difficult for us to cut ties.

I left her place, dejected. Yes, a Romeo was floored by a beautiful woman, all for nothing. A player had been played.

33

The uniform of play

I confess to suffering from a rare condition known as uniform fetish-ism. It is sexual in nature. According to Wikipedia, uniform fetishism is a sexual fetishism in which an individual is sexually aroused by uniforms. Yes, a uniform can aid in sexual matters. Well, it did for me. But that doesn't make me a jerk. All I am advocating is that all human beings in their diversity should be allowed to explore their rites of desire to the extent necessary and without impediments.

It should be noted that academic literature on uniforms as a fetish is sparse. Generally, the most common uniforms in the uniform-fetish category include those of a police officer, prison warder, soldier, schoolgirl and nurse.

Sociologists describe a person with a uniform fetish as someone who derives sexual pleasure from viewing others dressed in a typical uniform. In my case, my irrational obsession was with the South African Police Service (SAPS) uniform when worn by women. For me, it was also directly linked to the presence of a firearm.

Dr Dinesh Bhugra and Dr Padmal de Silva are two of a few researchers who have studied this phenomenon. Their 1996 paper looks at the function of uniforms, and their relationship with sexual fantasy and sexual fetishism. The authors note that uniforms can be seen as 'outer skins' that can be material and attractive in sexual terms, and that can enable individuals to display and wield power. They describe the functions of uniforms as comprising the five Fs: formal, fashion, fun, fantasy and fetish.

I feel something uniquely perplexing about the women in blue, and have had a desire to sleep with an armed woman dressed in the South African police uniform. I know it's wacky, but hear me out. My desire does not make me a masochist. I don't exhibit sexually deviant behaviour, so I don't associate the police uniform with punishment or torture as part of sexual pleasure.

My fetish for the women in blue is a long-standing condition. I became acutely aware of it in the early 1990s. The more women who joined the police service, the worse my condition became. I felt like a sexual deviant, but have realised I am not. In any event, many forms of sociologically deviant behaviour are not sanctioned by law, so I am not a sexual criminal either.

My sexual-uniform fetishism reached its crescendo in 1999, when I finally dated a cop. Yes, I was once in love with a woman to the extent that she was in a police uniform and brandished a gun. I must admit.

She wasn't my kind of girl: short, a little chubby and dark of complexion. As you know, I prefer my women tall, slender and yellow-boned.

I am certain that I was not sexually attracted to this particular woman beyond her wearing a police uniform. Let's put it this way: I was sexually attracted to her to the extent that she was a cop who wore a uniform and carried a gun. Our love affair, if you could call it that, was short-lived. But it was fun while it lasted. I had to cut it short because my uniform fetishism was wearing thin. She was an emotional being, in need of emotional excitement beyond her profession. I couldn't be there for her emotionally. I was not that into her.

In fact, I was into her to the extent that she was only allowed to come and see me during working hours, and – wait for it – she had to be in full police uniform and have her gun in its holster. As part of our play, my job was to disarm and undress her so that I could have my way with her. Clearly, this was not sustainable – at least for her. For me, it felt like having my cake and eating it too. I had the time of my life. I never disclosed my uniform fetish to her. She genuinely believed I was romantically attracted to her. Poor thing!

Our relationship ended abruptly. In her mind, she had fallen in love with me. However, for her to be certain, I had to pass an emotional test. She received manna from heaven when, in one of our sexual encounters, there was an incident in which the condom went kaput. Obviously, after the fact, we had to get an emergency contraceptive pill – which allowed us to play 'couple'. Weeks later, she told me she was pregnant. She also demanded that we both go for an HIV/AIDS test. However, every time we had an appointment to undergo the test, she didn't pitch. Any meeting with her became cumbersome, as she threatened to shoot herself if she discovered that I had infected her with HIV/AIDS.

A month later, in a bizarre confession, she admitted that she had just been playing games with my mind. She was neither HIV/AIDS-positive, nor pregnant, nor suicidal. 'I just wanted to see if you love me,' she said.

I had been in a panic, because I feared I might have contracted an STI – or HIV/AIDS. While I was relieved that she wasn't pregnant,

I couldn't forgive her for putting me through that emotional roller-coaster ride just to see if I loved her enough. The fact is, I was not in love with her, but in love with her police uniform. After this episode, my condition was somehow cured. I now look at police women as women, not just as objects of desire.

34

Hlengiwe: Lust and stolen virginity

Dear Hlengiwe

I received your letter dated 18 August 1993. I sincerely hope this response finds you well. I am sorry that it has taken me twenty-four years to write this letter to you. I am writing this to you to own up to my mis-demeanours of the past. Of late, I am haunted by memories of a dark past. In my dreams – or should we call them nightmares – I see you, and the many other women I have wronged, cry and beg me to explain my actions. When I wake up from the nightmares, the only thing buzz-ing in my ear is Adele's famous song 'Hello', and her line that she has not done much healing.

It is clear that there has to be a process of healing between us. I must atone for my lack of communication after all these years. I know I should have written to you earlier. There is no excuse for this, except the infamous lackadaisical manner in which I have always approached matters of the heart. But times are changing. When you wrote me your letter, I was half a man. I didn't have the guts to face up to my own frailty. I was a coward. I was what we refer to these days as trash.

Adele's song aside, I really want to know whether you made it out of KwaMaqwakazi. It was as boring as my village, eHabeni. I know that the only activities there, apart from hauling water from the dams, streams and rivers, were traditional ceremonies such as umembeso, umbondo and traditional weddings. Oh yes – I remember we also had a famous soccer team that always competed with your village's team. If my memory serves me well, we won most games. But I digress.

A lot has changed in the years since we last spoke. By the way, on my side, I did find love after what seemed like a lifetime of false starts. I refuse to say I am happily married. I prefer to say I am married. For better and for worse, I am no longer available on the open market. I am now a father to two beautiful children. I am a husband to a beautiful Englishwoman. Yes, I jumped off the cliff when it comes to marriage. I have since become more urbane and sensible; I must say, I live a very comfortable life in the formerly white suburbs here in Pretoria. So, I made it out of my village.

I also became a writer. Writing is a process I use to unburden myself and own up to my not-so-cosy past. Consider this letter a part of that process. Despite the rosy picture I have painted, I am not well – neither mentally nor physically. I live with a mental illness called major depressive disorder. I have had three surgeries since I turned forty. I am now beyond the age of the midlife crisis. Clearly, I am a man of advanced years; I will soon be turning fifty years old. I am told that fifty is beyond the age of redemption. Manly powers begin to wane. Again, I digress.

In your missive, you decry my behaviour during our last encounter. As I understand it, you decided to discontinue our dalliance barely a year after becoming my girlfriend. I am at my wits' end as I write this letter. For the better part of 1992, I pursued you with vigour because I had fallen in love with you. I must admit that this falling in love thingy was new for me. For all we know, it was just lust on steroids. At this hour, I have a confession to make. You are the only person to know *of this. You see, my previous girlfriends were nothing more than a collection to show off to my friends and prove that I was the man. But with you, it was different. There was something in your eyes and your smile that mellowed my heart. Your self-effacing demeanour was a real turn-on. Although we were young and naive, you showed me what it means to love and be loved. Despite the fact that you were extremely shy, whenever your spoke to me, you only ever spoke words of kindness. I even respected you for taking the time to consider my love proposal: it took me seven full months to convince you that I was serious. This should have been a clue that you were a woman of integrity – three times a lady, as it were.*

So, it is extremely difficult for me to process the emotions clearly articulated in your letter and to accept your decision, although I understand where you're coming from. I respect your decision. I should have believed you when you said you were a virgin. I didn't. For that, I am eternally sorry. At issue, though, is not just the lack of trust, but the fact that I stole your virginity in the bushes, of all places. Clearly, through my actions, I displayed the highest level of disrespect towards your bodily integrity. You obviously consider the violation of your bodily integrity as an infringement of ethics, intrusive and possibly criminal.

Let me repeat: I am sorry for my despicable behaviour. All I wish is to turn back time. However, I know that once the golden cup is broken, it can never be fixed. I am a bit older than you, so I should have known better. I allowed my high testosterone levels to rule the roost. Forgive me for the cliché that hormones can be blamed for everything.

In reality, I cannot begin to understand the magnitude of losing one's virginity in the manner in which you did. My actions were driven by lust and peer pressure, coupled with the deep-seated conservative and patriarchal tendencies of the time. I was a typical half a man, who behaved like trash. I cannot undo what happened between us. I wish it were a small matter that I could easily dismiss – about which I could say, 'Don't cry over spilled milk.' But it is not. It was your first sexual experience. You will never have it again. I stole your virginity in the name of love. You agreed to sleep with me because you were under pressure to prove that you loved me. In all honesty, you made it clear that you were not ready. I thought all the talk about not being ready was a ruse. You were left with little or no option but to accede to my incessant sexual demands. Of course, you didn't know better. You had no reference point.

I am sorry to have ruined your first sexual experience. To say it was not my intention would be to tell a lie. When I took that long trek from Durban to your school, I had one thing and one thing only on my mind – getting laid. I admit that I did realise early on during the sexual act that you were, indeed, a virgin, but by that time it was too late. I still feel like a thief who stole your innocence. There is no amount of forgiveness from you that would change these facts as we know them. There is no amount of remorse on my part that would alter the circumstances of how you lost your prized possession.

Again, I am sorry. I hope life has treated you well over the years. For what it's worth, I hope we can meet again to find closure. If we can't, I wish you well in your future endeavours.

I promise you that I am no longer half a man. I have grown to be a dependable father, husband and human being. Until we meet again –

Yours faithfully,
Bhekisisa Mncube

That's how I ought to have written back to Hlengiwe, my high-school sweetheart back in 1993. But I didn't. I read her three-page letter and was overcome with grief. Then I gave up on her. I gave up on what was possibly my first real love.

To humanise Hlengiwe, let me retell the story as it happened. I remember Hlengiwe as a beautiful woman by any measure. She was the 1990s version of today's yellow-bone phenomenon. I pursued her for the better part of 1992. So, when she finally said yes to my advances, I was thrilled. My diary entry records that day as 22 October 1992. Among my girlfriends at the time, she was definitely a leading light in the beauty stakes. I can say I may have felt some love for her. Look, in my early days of the courtship game, it was really difficult to separate lust from love. All roads led to Rome anyway.

Hlengiwe hailed from KwaMaqwakazi – a mere kilometre from our high school. The only snag was that she became my girlfriend a few weeks before the final matric exams, so I did not spend a lot of time with her while we were at school together. Our love affair blossomed via letters once I'd moved to Durban and she remained in high school. At some stage in 1993, I decided that it had been a long time since she had said yes to being my girlfriend, and that there had been no action between us, if you catch my drift. So, I took a taxi early on Friday morning and went straight to her high school, my alma mater. I waited at the school gate for the bell to ring. It was meant to be a surprise visit. She came out and found me waiting at the gate. We embraced, but no kissing. In those days, rural people had manners – no kissing or showing affection in public. I had one thing and one thing only on my mind. Sex. I explained my intentions in a roundabout way.

Look, it wasn't easy to bed a woman in those days. I lured her into the bushes under the pretext of having some privacy. After some fondling and kissing, I told her how much I wanted to score the ultimate prize. She told me that she was a virgin. Not for a minute did I believe her. After some gentle coaxing, I went the whole way and realised that she had been telling the truth all along. Immediately, I was overcome with grief. The whole scene was thoroughly embarrassing. I wish I had believed her. Two months later, I got her letter. She told me that the golden cup was broken – a euphemism for 'I no longer love you because you did not trust me and, of course, you violated me.'

I was sad to lose Hlengiwe, but there was no turning back.

Epilogue: The birth of a wordsmith

The year 2018 marks the eighteenth anniversary of the start of my official writing and publishing career. It all began in 2000, when my first article, on the merger of the Democratic Party (DP) and the New Nationalist Party (NNP), was published in the *Daily News* newspaper. The merger resulted in the launch of a new political party in South Africa, the Democratic Alliance (DA). The article ruffled a few feathers. It argued that this move was a step in the right direction to consolidate a strong opposition in the new South Africa. I held it up as a model that the Pan Africanist Congress (PAC) and Azanian People's Organisation (AZAPO) could follow in order to avoid inevitable political demise. My call to these two parties was not heeded, and we all know the outcome of that political intransigence.

Over the years, I have written extensively for the South African press, including for *The Witness, Weekend Witness,* Politicsweb, Bizcommunity.com, *Sunday Times (Lifestyle), The New Age, This Day, ANC Today, The Mirror, Witness/Echo, Public Eye, Mpumalanga Echo, Maritzburg Echo* (News24), *Edendale Echo* (Media24.com), *The Mercury, Sunday Tribune, The Independent on Saturday, Isolezwe, Daily News* and *Sunday World/Sowetan Sunday World*.

I have also written for the following magazines: *Transform SA,*

Bona and niche magazines of the University of Natal, such as *Focus* and *nuInTouch*. I have published in University of KwaZulu-Natal publications, including articles in *UKZNdaba*, *Development Brief* and *UKZNTouch*.

I contributed a chapter to the textbook *English First Additional Language FET Student's Book*, published by Macmillan Publishers South Africa (Pty) Ltd. I have also published in academic journals at home and abroad. These include *New Agenda: African Journal of Social and Economic Policy* and *Passages: A Chronicle of the African Humanities*, a journal of the University of Michigan, USA. I have also contributed to the University of KwaZulu-Natal publication *A Critical Engagement with Society*.

As a spokesperson/media liaison officer for various politicians, I have been featured or quoted in all major South African newspapers and on radio stations. I have featured regularly on television stations such as SABC News and Africa News Network7 (ANN7).

I serve as a Director of Speech Writing Services at the Department of Basic Education in Pretoria. I am the official speech writer to both the Basic Education Minister, Mrs Angie Motshekga, and her deputy, Mr Enver Surty. My speeches are regularly sent to all media for use in their news articles. I also write thought-leadership articles for the minister. I have, on various occasions, written speeches for President Jacob Zuma on basic-education-related matters. In 2016, my speech on the true state of basic education in South Africa featured as a front-page story in *City Press* newspaper. I have written a few speeches that have featured or been delivered live on all major South African television channels in the past three years. The same speeches were carried live on Power 98.7 FM, all SABC radio stations, and all community radio stations in South Africa.

I am also an Expert Author at EzineArticles.com, a peer-reviewed articles and marketing writers' ejournal in the USA, and a former member of the Book Review Panel at the *New Agenda* academic journal in South Africa. I remain on the list of book reviewers for the *Sunday Times*. For two and a half years, I was resident political analyst on Gagasi 99.5 FM and have featured on other radio stations such as SAfm, Power FM, Lotus FM, Radio Junto and Inanda 88.4 FM. I have provided political commentary to the following newspapers: *Business Day, Sunday Tribune, Isolezwe, Maritzburg Fever* and *The Times*. In 2012, I was listed as a preferred KwaZulu-Natal political analyst by the Al Jazeera English – Johannesburg Bureau.

Since November 2016, I have been a contributing columnist for *The Witness*, writing about what sociologists may call everyday life.

———

In 2001, I was appointed as a columnist for the *Witness/Echo* newspaper. My debut column called for the ANC to recall President Thabo Mbeki. It was a bold move, yet fraught with danger. It was only in 2008 that the ANC finally recalled Mbeki, for entirely different reasons. The column focused mainly on the political shenanigans of those who wielded power. My slogan at the time was 'a columnist worth his salt must write to raise hell'. The column ran for twelve years.

My first news story was published in *Sunday World* in 2001. It was about the IFP and the controversy its leader was causing by talking war in a democracy. I was not even employed by *Sunday World* at the time. In fact, I had arrived in Ulundi (my home town since 1997) to see my parents. I was intrigued by the large number of IFP supporters in town. I quickly learnt that they were attending the party's annual conference. I rushed to the venue at once, and arrived just in time to listen to the IFP leader's keynote address. After scribbling a few notes down on paper, it dawned on me that I had no computer or any means of communication to relay my story to Johannesburg. I took a quantum leap, and dialled the editor of *Sunday World* on the Telkom public phone. He phoned me back and I dictated the story to him. I soon became a regular freelancer for *Sunday World*.

In December 2001, I joined the Natal Witness Printing and Publishing Company as a cub reporter on the white suburbia supplement known as the *Mirror*. After paying my school fees as a cadet reporter, I was quickly moved up and appointed as a political reporter on the main paper, *The Witness*.

I resigned soon after my appointment to start my career in the corporate environment. I joined Mobile Telecommunications Network (MTN) as public relations officer for the Eastern Region (KwaZulu-Natal and Eastern Cape). During my stint at MTN (2002/03), I founded and edited *Bheki's Brief*, an electronic weekly telecommunications-industry newsletter.

Hardly three years later, I was back at *The Witness* as a senior political reporter. This move followed a stint at the University of KwaZulu-Natal as a writer/media liaison officer. I had been retrenched from MTN as part of their annual corporate restructuring.

In August 2005, I officially left journalism to join the KwaZulu-Natal Provincial Legislature. However, this was not of my own accord. My life had been threatened. The threats were made after the *Weekend Witness* published an exposé I had written as their front-page story. It detailed IFP leader Mangosuthu Gatsha Buthelezi's attempts to seize control of the Zulu royal house. The exposé came hot on the heels of a fervent State Intelligence-driven operation ahead of 2005's controversial 'Zulu Imbizo', an attempt to draw

KwaZulu-Natal back from the abyss of violent conflict. As part of the law-enforcement agencies' eleventh-hour efforts to avoid a bloodbath, Buthelezi's speech and the Imbizo's purported resolutions – written before it took place – were intercepted. Both were peppered with fighting talk. These two important documents were carefully leaked to me on a Friday night. As I was stationed in Pietermaritzburg, I had to rush to Durban, where an agent of the National Intelligence Agency (NIA) gave me an envelope full of goodies. I immediately telephoned my former deputy editor, Dr Yves Vanderhaeghen: 'Stop the presses, we have a scoop.'

He did exactly that. The next available opportunity to publish was in the *Weekend Witness*, a Saturday paper. Perfect. It coincided with the actual 'Zulu Imbizo'. The news scoop laid bare all of Buthelezi's plans, which amounted to the unilateral declaration of independence of the province.

On the same day, when I attended the Imbizo, I was attacked by the IFP's *impi*. I survived this attempt on my life. With the benefit of hindsight, I shouldn't have attended the Imbizo. I knew how it was all going to unfold. But, as a news junkie, I just couldn't miss a historic opportunity that would have far-reaching consequences for the province of KwaZulu-Natal in particular, and South Africa in general.

Legend has it that King Goodwill Zwelithini was so overjoyed by the publication of Buthelezi's shenanigans that he ordered every copy of the *Weekend Witness* in Nongoma to be bought and brought to eNyonkeni Palace.

When I resigned after this incident, I started a new career in the public service. I served as a spokesperson and speech writer to the KwaZulu-Natal Provincial Legislature's Speaker, Mr Willies Mchunu.

At the time of writing, he was serving as the premier of KwaZulu-Natal.

This was my first ANC deployment in a government sphere. The guy who made the call was the now late ANC spokesperson Mtholephi Mthimkhulu. May his gentle soul rest in peace!

I served Mr Mchunu for five long years in three separate state institutions: the KwaZulu-Natal Provincial Legislature, the Department of Local Government and Traditional Affairs, and the Departments of Transport, Community Safety and Liaison. At the KwaZulu-Natal Provincial Legislature, I founded and edited *Iso-Elibanzi*, the largest-circulating newspaper in the province of KwaZulu-Natal (500 000 copies) between 2005 and 2009.

In June 2010, my relationship with Mr Mchunu soured over the manner in which he was dealing with corruption committed before my arrival at the Departments of Transport, Community Safety and Liaison. I submitted, in confidence, an NIA document titled *The Villa – House of Horrors*. It detailed widespread corruption, including honey traps, illegal appointments, sex-for-jobs scandals and the use of state vehicles fitted with blue lights by some junior officials, to name just a few. When Mr Mchunu received this key document, he effectively stopped talking to me. Subsequently, he fired me via SMS on 1st July 2010. I challenged the dismissal at the Bargaining Chamber and lost. It was held that I had a one-year contract that had expired; this despite the fact that no such contract with my signature on it was ever produced. In fact, the respondent's attorneys conceded that no such contract existed.

Surprisingly, in a sworn affidavit, Mchunu said I had never been his spokesperson at the KwaZulu-Natal Provincial Legislature. He also claimed that he had had no relationship with me outside of the workplace. Both these assertions were untrue then, and are untrue now. Mchunu's legal representative said that he was not available to attend the arbitration hearing due to his heavy workload. His non-attendance robbed me of the opportunity to subject his sworn affidavit to cross-examination. Although I felt that justice was not done, I had to move on. So, no appeal was lodged.

Six months after being unceremoniously removed from Mchunu's ministerial office, I launched B74 Media Lab, a media and public-relations agency. I served as its founding managing director for almost three years. During my stint as a consultant, I did work for SA News, the South African government news agency, as KwaZulu-Natal free-lance political correspondent. As part of my duties at SA News, I did live reporting for GCIS Radio. I also wrote for the *Sunday Tribune* as a business correspondent. For eight months, I served as a public-relations manager at the Royal Household Trust, an agency of the KwaZulu-Natal provincial government charged with the overall management of the affairs of His Majesty, the King of the Zulus. I also had a stint as PR/media consultant to the European Union Delegation to South Africa, KwaZulu-Natal Provincial Legislature, and KwaZulu-Natal Department of Economic Affairs and Tourism, to name just a few.

In October 2013, I was redeployed by the ANC back to government. I served the MEC for the KwaZulu-Natal Department of Education, Ms Peggy Nkonyeni, as Director of Public Relations and Media Liaison. I effectively served as speech writer as well as a spokesperson. I left when my family relocated from Durban to Pretoria in June 2014. There, I was deployed in the Basic Education Ministry as Director of Speech Writing Services.

It still doesn't feel real that I made it out of my village of eHabeni and went beyond the Mpehlela mountains to settle comfortably in the administrative capital of South Africa, Pretoria. More often than not, I shudder to think of what happened to my childhood friends and acquaintances who never learnt what lay beyond those mountains. Today, I am living my childhood dream. I have my own family line, separate from that of my father. My son is an LLB varsity student, and my daughter has just started high school. I am grateful to those who have been part of my journey.

No one ever said it was going to be easy. But I made it. You can, too!

Acknowledgements

This book would not have been possible without the valuable insight and contribution of *The Witness* deputy editor, Ms Stephanie Saville. She ignited the fire inside me when she spotted a Facebook post and said to me, 'Hey, that could make a beautiful column.' Of course, she was talking about what has become the legendary story of Thabo, our not-so-new gardener. About 30 per cent of this book was first published in *The Witness* newspaper. I equally acknowledge the expeditious editing skills of *The Witness* features editor, Ms Linda Longhurst.

It will truly be an act of injustice if I don't mention my earlier mentors, to whom I owe my excellent grounding in journalism. These are the former editor of *The Witness* Mr John Conyngham, the newly appointed editor of *The Witness* Dr Yves Vanderhaeghen, former *Mirror* editor Ms Noelene Barbeau, former *Echo* editor Mr Bongani Mthethwa, and current *Echo* editor Mr Dumisane Zondi.

I acknowledge the tremendous work done by editors of Ezine-Articles.com, a peer-reviewed articles and marketing writers' ejournal in the US. At least 41 per cent of the articles in this book were also published there. The editors at EzineArticles worked tirelessly to ensure that my articles not only met their strict editorial guidelines, but contributed tremendously in ensuring that they were neither libellous nor overly controversial, and that they generally contained no offensive language.

I extend my appreciation to various websites that have re-published most of the stories in this collection.

I also wish to extend my sincere gratitude to two other persons: my wife, Professor D., and my daughter, Miss N. The story of my love life with Professor D. foregrounds most articles in this collection. My wife is the repository of my childhood dream of starting a humble family line separate from that of my father. Her love is true, pure and unselfish. Equally, my daughter is the pillar of our family: the body and pride of the Mncube clan. My firstborn son, Mr W., is one of a kind. He represents, through words and deeds, the values that underlie what it means to be human – to love, care, fail and succeed – all woven into a single person.

I also thank all my ex-girlfriends for inspiring me in various ways. My apologies for the fact that I am the kind of guy who kisses and tells. You have all defined and informed my long and sometimes arduous love life. I have abiding memories of ex-girlfriends who left me unexpectedly, those whose leaving was agonisingly slow and painful, and finally those whose love was greater for being unfulfilled. May the following ex-girlfriends rest in eternal peace: Thule, Thandiwe, Cebisile and Zodwa.

I am grateful to all my Facebook friends (all 2 386 of them) for their unwavering support and encouragement in the three years since this project began as *The Diaries of a Zulu Boy*. I cherish the number of times I was told, 'Write a book.' Well, here it is.

Towards the end of the arduous task of finalising this manuscript, I benefited generously from my intellectual sparring partners, Fred

Khumalo and Njabulo Mnyandu. In isiZulu we say, '*Ukwanda kwal-iwa umthakathi*.'

Overall, I am a recipient of human kindness. A man (a white male) gave me a lift in 1993. Yes, I was lost in the big city of Durban. My original intention was to get to the Technikon Natal Berea Campus. I ended up somewhere in Dalbridge. The man, whose name I never found out due to my limited English at the time, was busy in his shop, minding his own business, when in I came to ask for directions. He stopped whatever he was doing, went into his garage and drove me, in his Mercedes-Benz, to the right gate at Technikon Natal. I don't think saying thank you, sir, to him sufficed. I want to say in public that such human kindness should be acknowledged. I wouldn't be writing this today without that stranger's help.

Another white male – my comrade and political mentor, the late Derrick Anderson – taught me the principle of non-racialism. Another white comrade – this time of Afrikaner stock – and my fantasy lover, Ria Greyling, taught me the principle of non-homophobia.

But my biggest thank you, of course, is reserved for the people of Germany, who funded my education between 1991 and 2002. My greatest gratitude goes to all German taxpayers for their kindness and generosity. During the first year of my journalism studies, I was awarded the coveted Konrad-Adenauer-Stiftung International Scholarship. The scholarship is awarded to students and graduates of exceptional academic achievement and outstanding political or social commitment. Another stranger (I still don't know who it was), deposited R20 000 into my student account in 1999 to settle my old debt before the German scholarship kicked in. I would love to take this opportunity to say thank you, stranger, for your kindness.

I also acknowledge Ms Nalisha Kalideen. In 1999, Kalideen argued that I was more deserving of the scholarship than her, despite the fact that she was also a top student. She told the head of the journalism department that she was prepared to exclude herself from the shortlist in order for me to stand a better chance of being awarded the scholarship.

Today, I am a better person because of all these people – these fellow South Africans. I am prepared to die for any of them.

Equally, I thank my mom, Ntombikayise MaMlambo Mncube, for succeeding in raising seven children – including me – when the odds were heavily stacked against her. You're the body and soul of the Mncube family. Without you, we would truly be lost in the jungle of life.

But the real heroes and heroines of this book are the team at Penguin Random House, comprising my publisher, Marlene Fryer, managing editor Ronel Richter-Herbert, commissioning editor Melt Myburgh, and editor Angela Voges, who turned an ordinary manuscript into a real book. Angela, thanks for preserving my voice throughout the editing process. It was no easy task. You were absolutely awesome to work with.

Last but not least, I acknowledge, with humility, the help of my comrade, friend and brother, Mr Njabulo Mnyandu. Mr Mnyandu helped me draft a series of letters to Technikon Natal's intransigent senior management who had arbitrarily excluded me academically. With his help, we took the fight all the way to the council of the institution, which ruled in my favour. Folks, that's how it came to pass that I was admitted to undergraduate studies in journalism. Mr Mnyandu further read and commented on the earlier draft of the synopsis of this book. It is no exaggeration to say that, if it wasn't for the fighting spirit of Mr Mnyandu, and many others mentioned here, that you wouldn't be reading this book today.

Finally, I dedicate this body of work to my late big brother and

ACKNOWLEDGEMENTS

intellectual sparring partner, Bhekuyise Wilfred Mncube, the original Bheki. You were taken too soon. My dearest brother, you left us a rich legacy that will forever occupy a superior echelon of our minds and in our hearts. Your legacy of prioritising education, your love of reading and your selflessness is forever etched in our collective consciousness. Your legacy will not die while we live. Rest in eternal peace, Mzilankatha! We shall meet again.

Glossary of isiZulu terms

Amadlozi – ancestors, to whom we refer as *idlozi* in the singular; the human spirit or soul of the departed; regarded as still present and watching over the living

Amakhowe – the Zulu word for a species of edible mushroom that grows wild, mainly in subtropical habitats of southern Africa

Bhekisisa (Bheki) – my isiZulu name given to me by my father. Loosely translated, it means 'you must be vigilant'

Cebisile – a Zulu name for a girl child. It means 'the one who helps with a good idea'

Dololo – Zulu slang for 'nothing'

eHabeni – means 'place of hyperbole'. It is the village of my birth, in northern KwaZulu-Natal, near Eshowe

Fanakalo – a workplace lingua franca that has existed in South Africa for over a hundred years. It originated in the mines, and is a mixture of languages – isiZulu, English and Afrikaans

Hlonipha – means 'respect'

i-Straight – a main boyfriend in the context of multiple concurrent sexual partners

Icansi/amacansi – Zulu mats

Imbeleko – means a Zulu cultural ceremony wherein a goat is slaughtered to celebrate the newly born in the family and to officially introduce him or her to the ancestors

Impepho – a small plant with a sweet smell, burned as an offering to the spirits of the departed

Impi – a body of Zulu warriors

Ishende – a secret lover in the context of multiple concurrent sexual partners

Isibaya – a kraal; an area typically enclosed by tree logs, where livestock is kept overnight and where important ceremonies, such as the slaughter of domestic animals, take place

Isicholo – a Zulu head-covering for married women and brides

Isidikiselo – a secondary lover in the context of multiple concurrent sexual partners

Isidwaba – a Zulu skirt made from cow hide, for married women

Isifebe – a woman with multiple concurrent sexual partners

Isoka lamanyala – a man with multiple concurrent sexual partners

Isigodlo – a palace of the *Inkosi* or chief and/or king

Isinamuva liyabukwa – an isiZulu idiom loosely translated to mean 'he who dances last gets all the attention'

Isiphandla – an armlet of goat hide that is worn by the particular person for whom the goat was slaughtered. It is worn for many traditional purposes by Africans, especially Zulus, who practise their tradition and belief in ancestors

Izibizo – gifts expressly requested by the bride's family to be paid for by the groom

Izithakazelo – the praise name of a clan to show *inhlonipho* (respect) and to recognise important clan members who came before the descendant, the forebears. It is always attached to a particular descent group

Khuluma – to talk

Lobola – a dowry required before nuptials, to be paid by the groom. It is prevalent among Zulus and other tribes in southern Africa, and is generally paid by the groom in cattle to the bride's family. Nowadays, most families accept cash in lieu of cows

Makoti – bride

Mama – mother

Mjondolo – a house built with inappropriate materials, located in an informal settlement. It is sometimes referred to as a shack

Mlungu – colloquial term for a white person

Mzilankatha – the Mncubes' praise name

Nompilo – a Zulu name for a girl child. It means 'the one who brings life'

Sasidla imbuya ngothi – literally translated, 'we were eating grass with a stick'. It means living in abject poverty

Sawubona – hello

Sebenzile – a Zulu name for a girl child. It means 'you have worked hard to bring joy to the family'

Thokoza Dlozi – a chant made during a consultation with *isangoma* (a traditional healer or seer)

Ubaba – father

Ukubuyisa – to return the spirit of the dead home

Ukuchithwa kwegazi – the spilling of blood or slaughtering of an animal during a Zulu cultural ceremony

Ukukhumelana umlotha – a traditional Zulu form of reconciliation (a peace-making ritual)

Ukuphulula imbuzi – to stroke or rub a goat very gently while the elder of the family is communicating with ancestors

Ukuphupha – to dream while asleep

Ukuthetha idlozi – a sacred Zulu tradition of communication between the ancestors and their descendants

Ukuyala – loosely translated, this means 'to advise'. It is an important ritual that occurs on the second day of the traditional wedding. Elders from the bride's and groom's families meet the newlyweds for a serious chat about *hlonipha* and other matters that will make the union strong

Ukuyomlanda – going to the place where the deceased took his or her last breath

Ukuzalwa wembethe – to be born with a veil, caul or hood covering one's face

Ukuzila – a process of mourning one's beloved, especially a husband, in a culturally determined way, such as wearing black clothing for a predetermined period

Ukwanda kwaliwa ngumthakathi – a Zulu proverb meaning 'a wicked heart hates it when others succeed'

Ukwenana – a cultural form of exchange where the recipient accepts, intending to return or reciprocate in kind, but in which the giver engages knowing that there may not, in fact, be reciprocation

Ukushweleza emadlozini – a ceremony held to ask ancestors to repel imminent danger or offer an apology for a particular significant cultural transgression

Umabo – similar to *umembeso* in the sense that these are bespoke gifts ordered by the groom's family to be delivered on the day of the traditional wedding

Umbondo – a ceremony in which the bride reciprocates *izibizo* by buying a variety of gifts for the groom's family

Umembeso – a Zulu ceremony in which the groom's family takes gifts to the bride's family to say thank you for the gift of their new daughter-in-law. It is important to note that the purpose of *umembeso* is to show the future wife how the in-laws want her to dress as their future daughter-in-law

uMlahlankosi – a sacred tree for taking the spirit of the dead home

Umqombothi or utshwala – Zulu beer

Umsamo – a sacred place inside a hut where communication between the living and the ancestors takes place. Generally located away from the doorway of the hut, it is where things like beer pots are placed and also where a goat is hung after it has been slaughtered and skinned

uMvelinqangi – the African God of Creation – 'the one who came first'

uNgamla – a colloquial term for a white man

Uphuthu – dry mealie-meal porridge favoured in KwaZulu-Natal (as opposed to pap, which is also known as *mieliepap* – Afrikaans for 'maize porridge' – in South Africa, *sadza* in Shona, or *isitshwala* in the isiNdebele language in Zimbabwe

Zodwa – a shortened version of Ntombizodwa, a Zulu name for a girl child. It means 'we have another girl child'

Notes for further reading

BOOKS

Brink, André. (2004) *Before I Forget.* UK: Secker & Warburg

Coetzee, J.M. (1977) *In the Heart of the Country.* USA: Harper
& Row

Forward, Susan. (2002) *Toxic Parents: Overcoming Their Hurtful
Legacy and Reclaiming your Life.* USA: Penguin Random House

Paton, Alan. (1948) *Cry, the Beloved Country.* USA: Scribners

OTHER SOURCES

A Traditional Zulu Marriage – My African Heritage. Accessed
on 20 June 2017 from http://www.myafricanheritage.com/
subpage.html

Claire Lisa Jaynes. (2007) 'Interracial Intimate Relationships in
Post-apartheid South Africa'. Thesis, Master of Arts in Com-
munity-based Counselling, University of the Witwatersrand.
·Accessed on 24 August 2017 from http://wiredspace.wits.ac.za/
bitstream/handle/10539/4905/JAYNESCL_Research%20report.
pdf?sequence=2 Stages in a Zulu Wedding: Umembeso I The
Ulwazi Programme. Accessed on 20 June 2017 from https://
www.google.co.za/#q=umembeso+&spf=1497976019812

Interview with my mother, Ntombikayise MaMlambo Mncube, 20 June 2017.

Interview with my mother-in-law, 14 August 2017.

Thobekile Patience Luthuli. (2007) 'Assessing politeness, language and gender in hlonipha'. Thesis, Master's Degree in Languages, Linguistics and Academic Literacy, UKZN. Accessed on 20 June 2017 from https://researchspace.ukzn.ac.za/handle/10413/1567

Thobile Thandiwe Ngcongo. (1996) 'Orality and transformation in some Zulu ceremonies: Tradition in transition'. Thesis, Master's Degree in Languages and Arts Education, UKZN. Accessed on 28 July 2017 from https://researchspace.ukzn. ac.za/handle/10413/7079

Tiny Happy Sarah Setsiba. (2012) 'Mourning Rituals and Practices in Contemporary South African Townships: A Phenomenological Study'. Thesis, Doctoral Degree in Community Psychology, Department of Psychology, University of Zululand. Accessed on 28 July 2017 from http://uzspace.uzulu.ac.za/bitstream/ handle/10530/1055/MOURNING%20RITUALS%20AND%20 PRACTICES%20IN%20CONTEMPORARY%20SOUTH%20 AFRICAN%20TOWNSHIPS.pdf?sequence=1

Umbondo | The Ulwazi Programme. Accessed on 20 June 2017 from https://www.google.co. za/#q=umbondo&spf=1497976195314

Zulu traditional wedding – umabo | eNanda Online. Accessed on 20 June 2017 from http://enanda.co.za/2013/07/zulu-traditional-wedding-umabo/

CHAPTER 1

This article was first published as follows:

Mncube, B. (2017) Dark Secret Revealed: I Was Molested as a
Child. 9 February 2017. Accessed on 16 March 2017 from
http://ezinearticles.com

CHAPTER 2

A shortened version of this article was first published as follows:

Mncube, B. (2017) Mixing Bodies and Cultures: Love, Race and
Prejudice. 22 February 2017. Accessed on 16 March 2017 from
http://ezinearticles.com

Mncube, B. (2017) Mixing Bodies and Cultures: Love, Race and
Prejudice. 27 March 2017. Accessed on 27 March 2017 from
www.marvin.co.za

Mncube, B. (2017) Mixing Bodies and Cultures: Love, Race and
Prejudice. 28 February 2017. Accessed on 27 March 2017 from
www.theblacklist.net

CHAPTER 3

The shortened version of this article was first published as follows:

Mncube B. (2015) Whiteness and I. Politicsweb, 11 November
2015. Accessed on 16 March 2017 from www.politicsweb.co.za

CHAPTER 6

This article was first published as follows:

Mncube, B. (2017) Four Weddings Down and Three More to Go.
The Witness, 26 January 2017, p. 15.

Mncube, B. (2017) Four Weddings and Counting. 19 January
2017. Accessed on 16 March 2017 from http://ezinearticles.com

Mncube, B. (2017). Four Weddings Down, Three More to Go.
27 January 2017. Accessed on 28 March 2017 from http://
internetdo.com/technology/four-weddings-and-counting.html
This article was also published on Facebook on 26 January 2017.

CHAPTER 8
This article was first published as follows:
Mncube, B. (2017) Introducing an English wife to my Zulu
ancestors. *The Witness*, 4 May 2017, p. 11.
Mncube, B. (2017) Introducing an English wife to my Zulu
ancestors. 9 May 2017. Accessed on 10 May 2017 from
www.marvin.co.za
Mncube, B. (2017) I'm Done with Weddings, and Weddings
Are Done. 19 April 2017. Accessed on 5 May 2017 from
http://ezinearticles.com/
This article was also published on Facebook on 4 May 2017.

CHAPTER 13
This article was published on Facebook on 2 February 2017.

CHAPTER 14
This article was first published as follows:
Mncube, B. (2016) Bizarre Case of Thabo and Garden of Eden.
30 November 2016. Accessed on 16 March 2017 from
http://ezinearticles.com
Mncube, B. (2016) Bizarre Case of Thabo and Garden of Eden.
The Witness, 23 November 2016, p. 9.
It was also published on Facebook in various incarnations.
A longer version was published on 16 September 2015.

CHAPTER 15

This article was first published as follows:

Mncube, B. (2016) Pool and Bean Boys Put Writer's Marriage on the Rocks. 6 December 2016. Accessed on 16 March 2017 from http://ezinearticles.com

Mncube, B. (2016) Pool and Bean Boys Put Marriage on the Rocks. *The Witness*, 5 December 2016, p. 9.

A shortened version was published on Facebook on 20 November 2014.

CHAPTER 17

This article was first published as follows:

Mncube, B. (2017) I Cheat, Therefore I Am. 2 February 2017. Accessed on 16 March 2017 from http://ezinearticles.com

CHAPTER 18

This article was first published as follows:

Mncube, B. (2017 Sex-Less Relationship 101. 8 February 2017. Accessed on 16 March 2017 from http://ezinearticles.com

Mncube, B. (2017) A Polyandrous Relationship Goes South. *The Witness*, 24 February 2017, p. 9.

A series of shortened versions of this article was posted on Facebook on 22 January 2015 and 9 August 2016.

CHAPTER 19

This article was first published as follows:

Mncube, B. (2017) Her Love was True and Unselfish. *The Witness*, 17 February 2017, p. 9.

Mncube, B. (2017) True love. 1 March 2017. Accessed on 28 March 2017 from http://www.news24.com/SouthAfrica/Local/Maritzburg-Fever/true-love-20170222-2

A shortened version of this article was posted on Facebook on
9 August 2016.

CHAPTER 20
This article was first published as follows:
Mncube, B. (2017) Valentine's Day: 14 Roses and a Funeral. 3 March
2017. Accessed on 3 March 2017 from http://ezinearticles.com

CHAPTER 21
This article was first published as follows:
Mncube, B. (2017) Zodwa: My Greatest First Love. 15 February
2017. Accessed on 16 March 2017 from http://ezinearticles.com
Mncube, B. (2017) Zodwa: My Greatest First Love. 27 February
2017. Accessed on 28 March 2017 from http://atozrelationships.
com/zodwa-my-greatest-first-love/
A shortened version of this article was posted on Facebook on
20 November 2014.

CHAPTER 23
This article was first published as follows:
Mncube, B. (2017) True Love: True Betrayal and a Baby Boy.
Accessed on 17 July 2017 from http://ezinearticles.com/

CHAPTER 24
This article was first published as follows:
Mncube, B. (2017) The Challenge of Pleasure: Re-Imagining
Sexuality and Consent. 14 February 2017. Accessed on
16 March 2017 from http://ezinearticles.com

CHAPTER 25

This article was first published as follows:

Mncube, B. (2017) Busi: Toxic Masculinity and Gender Based
Violence. 15 February 2017. Accessed on 16 March 2017 from
http://ezinearticles.com

A shortened version was posted on Facebook on 19 June 2016.

CHAPTER 26

A three-part series of this article was published on Facebook
during the month of September and October 2016. Part one:
7 September 2016; Part two: 7 October 2016; Part three:
17 October 2016.

It was also published as a full-length article as follows:

Mncube, B. (2016) Lindiwe: Antics of a Crazy Ex-Girlfriend.
6 December 2016. Accessed on 16 March 2017 from http://
ezinearticles.com

CHAPTER 29

This article was first published as follows:

Mncube, B. (2017) Stranger in My Bed: Love, Lust and Obsession.
3 March 2017. Accessed on 16 March 2017 from http://
ezinearticles.com

CHAPTER 30

This article was first published as follows:

Mncube, B. (2017) Date My Family: Love, Lust and Jealousy.
14 March 2017. Accessed on 23 March 2017 from
http://ezinearticles.com

CHAPTER 33

This article was first published as follows:

Mncube, B. (2017) The Uniform of Play: Gun and Police Uniform as an Object of Sexual Desire. 9 March 2017. Accessed on 16 March 2017 from http://ezinearticles.com

Mncube, B. (2017) The Uniform of Play: Gun and Police Uniform as an Object of Sexual Desire. 17 March 2017. Accessed on 28 March 2017 from http://education2web.blogspot.co. za/2017/03/the-uniform-of-play-gun-and-police.html